SOCIOLOGY SINCE 1995
Volume 1

Jonathan Blundell and Janis Griffiths

Published by Connect Publications,
Cooksbridge House, Cooksbridge,
Lewes, East Sussex BN8 4SR
Telephone 01273 401714
E-mail: connect.pub@mistral.co.uk

First published 2002
ISBN 0 9520683 9 7

This book is based on an original idea by Hazel Manuel

Editorial and project management: Peter Langley
Design: Patricia Briggs
Copy editing: Carol Schaessens
Cover: Tony Ashton
Thanks to Warren Kidd
Printing: The Print House, Hove

Every effort has been made to trace the copyright holders, but if any have been inadvertently overlooked the publishers will be pleased to make the necessary acknowledgement at the first opportunity.
　　The publishers grant permission for multiple copies of any material from this book to be made within the place of purchase for use solely within that institution.

CONTENTS

Introduction	v
Methods matching chart	vi
Section 1: **EDUCATION**	1
Section 2: **RELIGION**	29
Section 3: **MASS MEDIA**	47
Section 4: **AGE AND YOUTH CULTURE**	68
Section 5: **GENDER**	88
Section 6: **POVERTY AND WELFARE**	112

INTRODUCTION

USING THIS BOOK *Sociology since 1995* is designed to fulfil a range of needs for teachers and students of Sociology.

> **1 Keeping up to date**
> Teachers can use the book to help them keep abreast of recent research in the topics they cover. Interesting and relevant contemporary examples can be provided which should help motivate students and enhance the quality of teaching and learning. Use the table provided to see at a glance the central issues dealt with by each summary.
>
> **2 Methods teaching**
> The studies cover all of the main methods and research approaches used by sociologists. They provide excellent contemporary examples of real research in action, showing how sociologists deal with the problems of choosing methods, conducting research, presenting data and interpreting their findings. A table is provided to allow users of the book to find examples of the use of particular methods and approaches.
>
> **3 Coursework**
> The book can be used to help students with the coursework requirements of either board at both AS and A2 level. The summaries can be used as Contexts for AQA AS level coursework and as the basis for OCR Research Reports. They also provide accessible secondary sources for A2 coursework studies.

SELECTION OF THE STUDIES The studies included have been chosen to represent the full range of methods and approaches and to reflect some of the key concerns of Sociology today. Many cover issues which are of direct relevance and interest to young people. An attempt has been made to include original and unusual studies which cast new light on some familiar debates and themes.

Teachers and students are encouraged to seek out the original publication where they have a particular interest. The summaries give some idea of the accessibility of the original on which they are based and teachers should bear this in mind when considering purchase of the source material.

ORGANISATION OF THE SUMMARIES Each study is summarised and discussed under the same headings: Context, Methods, Findings, Importance and Evaluation. Questions focusing on understanding and analysis skills follow each study. The Evaluation section and the questions are placed on a separate side wherever possible so teachers do not need to issue these to students. This means that students can be set the task of evaluating the study themselves if this is thought appropriate.

VOLUME 2 *Sociology since 1995* is the first of two volumes which consist of summaries of recent empirical research. The second volume will consist of the following topics:
- *Families and households*
- *Crime and deviance*
- *Race and ethnicity*
- *Social class and inequality*
- *Health*
- *Politics and protest.*

METHODS MATCHING CHART

EDUCATION

	TITLE	AUTHOR(S)	PUBLISHER	DATE
p. 1	Social Class and Higher Education: Issues Affecting Decisions on Participation by Lower Social Class Groups	H. Connor and S. Dewson with C. Tyers, J. Eccles, J. Regan, J. Aston	Institute for Employment Studies, HMSO	2001
p. 6	Rationing Education: Policy, Practice, Reform and Equity	D. Gillborn and D. Youdell	Open University Press	2000
p. 10	Markets, Choice and Equity in Education	S. Gewirtz, S.J. Ball, R. Bowe	Open University Press	1995
p. 15	Divide and School	J. Abraham	Falmer Press	1995
p. 20	Black Masculinities and Schooling	T. Sewell	Trentham Books	1997
p. 25	Improving School Effectiveness	J. MacBeath and P. Mortimore	Open University Press	2001

RELIGION

	TITLE	AUTHOR(S)	PUBLISHER	DATE
p. 29	Islam in Transition: Religion and Identity among British Pakistani Youth	J. Jacobson	Routledge	1998
p. 33	The Emerging Network: A Sociology of the New Age and Neo-Pagan Movements	M. York	Rowman and Littlefield	- 1995
p. 37	'Neither Here nor There': The Construction of Identities and Boundary Maintenance of West African Pentecostals	S. Hunt	Sociology, Volume 36 Number 1	Feb. 2001
p. 42	The Kendal Project: Patterns of the Sacred in Contemporary Society	Department of Religious Studies at Lancaster University	Unpublished work in progress	N/A

MASS MEDIA

	TITLE	AUTHOR(S)	PUBLISHER	DATE
p. 47	TV Living	D. Gauntlett, A. Hill	Routledge	1999
p. 51	Dear BBC	M. M. Davies	Cambridge University Press	2001
p. 55	Viewing the World	Dept. for International Development	DID	2000
p. 60	Message Received	G. Philo (ed)	Addison Wesley Longman	1999
p. 64	Frock Rock	M. Bayton	Oxford University Press	1998

Issues	Methods
• What factors affect the decision to go to university among those from lower social class backgrounds? • How is the decision-making process different for different types of people? • What can be done to improve the number of people from less wealthy backgrounds going on to higher education?	• Group and individual interviews • Postal questionnaires
• How have teachers and pupils been affected by educational change? • How has educational change affected equality in schools?	• Qualitative: observation and interviews
• What have been the effects of the introduction of a consumer market into education? • How much choice do parents really have?	• Semi-structured interviews • Quantitative and qualitative secondary data
• How are class and gender divisions reinforced by the school? • How does the school reproduce social differences?	• Structured observation • Questionnaires • In-depth interviews • Qualititative secondary data
• How do schools oppress African-Caribbean boys? • How do the boys respond to this oppression?	• Semi-structured interviews • Observation
• How can the quality of schools be judged? • What makes an effective school?	• Surveys using questionnaires • Case studies: observation and interviews

Issues	Methods
• How is the identity of young British Pakistanis shaped by their Islamic faith?	• Semi-structured interviews • Unstructured intreviews • Observation
• What attracts people to the New Age and Neo-pagan movements? • Do the New Age and Neo-pagan movements fit into existing typologies of sects and cults?	• Observation • Participant observation • Questionnaires • Secondary data
• Why does Pentecostalism appeal to Nigerians in Britain? • How do they use it to help construct identities?	• Semi-structured group and individual interviews • Content analysis
• What is the extent of religious belief and participation in Kendal? • Which theory about the state of religion in contemporary Britain is most relevant?	• Case study involving a range of quantitative and qualitative methods

Issues	Methods
• How do people watch TV? • What does TV mean to different groups of people? • What media issues are the public concerned about?	• Longitudinal survey • Diaries
• What do children think about TV? • What effects does TV have on children? • How do the media cover the less-developed world?	• Questionnaires • Discussion tasks
• How does media coverage affect people's attitudes to the less-developed world? • What do programme makers feel about their role in covering development issues?	• Content analysis • Group and individual interviews
• How do children react to violence in the media? • How did media reporting of BSE affect public attitudes? • How did the media cover the 1994 Rwanda crisis?	• Individual and group interviews • Thematic (content) analysis
• How do women get involved in rock music? • What problems are faced by women in rock music?	• Informal interviews • Participant observation

AGE AND YOUTH CULTURE

	Title	Author(s)	Publisher	Date
p. 68	Club Cultures	S. Thornton	Polity Press	1995
p. 72	Clubbing: Dancing, Ecstasy and Vitality	B. Malbon	Routledge	1999
p. 76	Inside Subculture	D. Muggleton	Berg	2000
p. 80	Metal Heads	J.J Arnett	Westview Press	1996
p. 84	The Family and Community Life of Older People	C. Phillipson, M. Bernard, J. Phillips, J. Ogg	Routledge	2001

GENDER

	Title	Author(s)	Publisher	Date
p. 88	Uncertain Masculinities	M. O'Donnell, S. Sharpe	Routledge	2000
p. 92	The Company She Keeps	V. Hey	Open University Press	1997
p. 97	Formations of Class and Gender	B. Skeggs	Sage Publications	1997
p. 102	Marketing Molly and Melville	E. Jagger	Sociology Vol 35 no. 1	2001
p. 107	Women, Violence and Male Power	M. Hester, L. Kelly, J. Radford	Open University Press	1996

POVERTY AND WELFARE

	Title	Author(s)	Publisher	Date
p. 112	A Study of Town Life: Living Standards in the City of York 100 Years after Rowntree	M. Huby, J. Bradshaw and A. Corden	Joseph Rowntree Foundation	1999
p. 118	Breadline Britain in the 1990s	D. Gordon and C. Pantazis (eds)	Ashgate Publishing	1997
p. 122	Poverty and Social Exclusion in Britain	D. Gordon, L. Adelman, K. Ashworth, J.Bradshaw, R. Levitas, S. Middleton, C. Pantazis, D. Patsios, S. Payne, P. Townsend, J. Williams	Joseph Rowntree Foundation	2000
p. 126	The Impact of Childhood Disability on Family Life	Barbara Dobson, Sue Middleton and Alan Beardsworth	Joseph Rowntree Foundation	2001

Issues	Methods
• What is subcultural capital and what role does it play in club culture? • What is clubbing like?	• Participant observation • Unstructured interviews • Qualitative secondary data
• What does clubbing mean to people?	• Unstructured interviews
• Do people move between subcultures? • What is the relationship between subcultures and postmodernity?	• Semi-structured interviews
• What role does heavy metal music play in the lives of its fans?	• Semi-structured interviews • Questionnaires • Content analysis
• What is family and community life like for older people? • What changes have taken place since the mid twentieth century?	• Questionnaires • Unstructured interviews

Issues	Methods
• How are the identities of young males created? • Are boys a problem for society?	• Questionnaires • Unstructured interviews
• How do teenage girls create their identities? • How do young females negotiate their friendships with other girls?	• Participant observation
• How do gender and class overlap in the lives of working class women?	• Longitudinal study • Participant observation • Feminist methodologies
• How do advertisers in the personal pages of newspapers and magazines create identities? • How do these identities relate to traditional gender stereotypes?	• Content analysis
• How do different groups of women experience different types of male violence?	• Feminist methodologies

Issues	Methods
• How can Rowntree's classic study of poverty in York be updated? • How much poverty is there in York today and how does it affect people?	• Semi-structured interviews • Secondary data • Sample survey
• What do people believe to be essential in modern Britain? • How many people live in poverty using this consensual definition? • How do poor people live?	• Structured interviews • Official statistics
• How much poverty exists in Britain? • Who is vulnerable to poverty? • What is the relationship between poverty and social exclusion?	• Structured interviews
• What are the financial costs for parents of children with a severe disability? • Do parents receive sufficient financial support to help them take on caring duties? • What are the emotional costs of bringing up a child with a disability? • How do families adjust when they gain a disabled member?	• Group interviews • Questionnaires • Diaries

SOCIOLOGY SINCE 1995

SOCIAL CLASS AND HIGHER EDUCATION
ISSUES AFFECTING DECISIONS ON PARTICIPATION BY LOWER SOCIAL CLASS GROUPS

Helen Connor and Sara Dewson with Claire Tyers, Judith Eccles, Jo Regan, Jane Aston

Institute for Employment Studies, Department for Education and Employment Studies, HMSO, March 2001

CONTEXT

Since the 1960s there has been a huge expansion of higher and further education in Britain. Despite the opportunities that now present themselves to people of all backgrounds to study at a higher level, there remain very large differences in participation rates. Many universities have policies that attempt to widen access from people of different backgrounds. In over forty years, however, the participation rate has only increased from 3% of people in 1950 to 17% in 1998. The authors of the report note that in certain areas, such as those of gender and ethnicity, there has been a widening of participation, but this does not extend to social class differentials. 45% of people who come from higher social classes tend to take up courses that lead to higher educational qualifications; this contrasts with a less than 20% take-up among the lower social classes. In certain subjects and institutions, the participation of lower social-class groupings can be as low as 10%, though in others it may rise to 40%. In late 1999, the Department for Education and Employment (DfEE) commissioned this research in order to understand in more detail the factors influencing people of lower social-class backgrounds in their decision to go to university.

This research took place in the context of major changes to the funding of students who choose to undertake higher education. Whereas before the 1990s students were often given grants to attend university, by the time this study was undertaken students were expected to contribute to their own funding via cheap loans. Many students leave university carrying a burden of debt that they are expected to pay off through their increased life-earnings as graduates.

METHODS

The research focused on groups of people who were qualified, or on the point of qualifying, for higher education. This meant that the decision-making process itself became the primary focus of study. Obvious questions about the failure of all members of lower social groups to participate in higher education study would be beyond the brief of a single research team.

The Methods Appendix of this survey merits further attention from anyone studying sociological methods because of the detail offered about the research process and the clear explanations of the choices that the research team made.

The aims of the study are clearly stated. They were to:

- explore factors that encourage or prohibit participation in higher education by students from lower social-class groups.
- assess the relative important of these factors for different sub-groups of students (e.g. ethnic-minority groups, mature students, with different entry qualifications, studying different subjects of types of courses).
- make appropriate policy recommendations.

There were three groups of respondents.

1. **Potential entrants** who were those in post-16 education on courses that would lead to university entry-level qualifications. 223 students from 20 colleges and schools in England and Wales on A-level, BTEC, GNVQ and Access courses participated in 29 focus groups. These were predominantly young, but there were some Access-course students who were older. One-third of this group came from minority-ethnic backgrounds. Two-thirds of the students were female. Geographically, they were drawn from targeted regions: the north of England, the East Midlands, London and South Wales. The majority of students had already decided to go on to further education.

2. **Current students** in higher education. These students came from higher and lower social-class groupings. They were questioned by a large postal survey with follow-up interviews. A sample of institutions were selected according 'to type and geographical location' and then a sample was selected at each institution according to social class. Fourteen institutions were approached: an older university, a newer university or a college of higher education in each region. Four further education colleges with large numbers of higher education students were contacted. Nearly 4,000 questionnaires were sent out and 41% were returned. The total number of actual responses was 1,677, of which 574 could not be identified to a type of institution. There were 20 follow-up interviews with respondents on full-time courses. These were chosen on the basis of: age, disability, ethnic-minority status and lone parents.

3. **Non-HE students** were those from lower-class backgrounds who did not choose to enter HE but who have qualifications that make them eligible for higher education. This study group was difficult to identify and contact so the description of the method used makes interesting reading. They were identified from a previous sequence of studies conducted by the National Opinion Poll (NOP) and contacted via telephone. 176 people were contacted, but a proportion of these were now in higher education and so invalidated from the survey. Only 112 interviews were achieved despite there being a higher target. The majority of these were in employment, but some were in work-based training. There was one unemployed person and a small number of people who were looking after children.

KEY FINDINGS

The report uses the terms 'higher' and 'lower social-class grouping' throughout. The class system used is that used in most governmental research which is known as 1992 Standard Occupational Coding. Classes I, II and III non-manual were agreed to be higher social classes and Classes III manual, IV and V were agreed to be lower. The allocation of class was on the basis of father's occupation – if no father, then mother, and then own occupation. There are issues with this operationalisation of the concept of class that the study group acknowledge, but as most secondary data uses this classification then the findings of this research could be more closely integrated with data already gathered by official groups such as UCAS.

Students are influenced in their decision to participate in higher education by a range of factors including the following.

- Entry qualifications and school experience.
- Family background and support.
- Financial factors.
- Institutional factors relating to access and recruitment policies of the universities and colleges.

Lower social-class groupings are under-represented in higher education. Not only are they under-represented, but this is a continuation of a long-standing pattern of social exclusion. This is despite 50 years of legislation that attempted, at least in theory, to make Britain a more equal and meritocratic society where people progress on the basis on ability and not wealth.

There is uneven distribution of social classes across the higher education sector, in particular by institution and by subject choice. Lower-class students are less likely to be found on degree courses, and more likely to be on HND courses than higher-class students. They are less likely to be found in traditional universities and more likely to be discovered in institutes of higher education. There is a tendency for them to apply to their nearest colleges, particularly if they are mature students. Lower-class males are more likely to find their way onto engineering courses, but females tend to target business and social sciences. This reflects patterns in male and female employment.

Low rates of participation among lower social classes are due to the following factors.

- **Educational background and qualifications**. Students from lower-class backgrounds are likely to have difficulty in achieving entry qualifications. Fewer students from poor backgrounds achieve two or more A-levels and many non-traditional vocational qualifications such as GNVQ are not highly regarded by universities, despite their being popular with students.
- **Family background and geographical location**. Parental education levels can affect students. Affluent parents have the means and the knowledge to support children in school. Children who live in wealthy areas and attend schools in those areas have a higher likelihood of attending university.
- **Affording the costs of further study**. Many students feared debt. Students were also concerned that they would need to have work in order to support further study.

Lower-class students entering higher education are more likely to be mature students who enter universities via the Access course route.

Qualitative evidence taken from interviews makes interesting reading. Lower-class students were slightly more likely to go to college to increase earning potential, whereas higher-class students were attracted to a specific subject area. It is clear from this study that financial considerations exert both a pull and a push factor in the decision of lower social classes to attend higher education. The pull factor is the possibility of better and more interesting jobs or highly paid work. Other social factors include confidence and independence. The push factor away from higher education was the risk of specific financial difficulty. Single parents, for instance, feared loss of benefits. Interestingly, not all of the people who rejected higher education accepted the common view that a degree leads to a better job. Many felt that even if they gained higher level qualifications, they would not necessarily improve their employment prospects. One referred to the previous experience of a sister who had three jobs to support her studies and had also acquired a 'huge overdraft'.

Lower-class students often had negative experiences of school and had seen no point in their studies. They were therefore influenced in their desire to participate by family members or friends. Careers education in schools was considered to be less than helpful in advising potential students. Lower-class students felt particularly in need of advice at this stage. Gender and relationship dynamics were important in the decision to progress to higher education for lower-class students. Some female students had faced problems with their partner, whereas there was no opposition from the partners of male students.

The chapter on student finance and funding is enormously important and extremely detailed in its analysis of student funding and attitudes towards to debt. Many students made decisions about their future educational progress on the basis of finance. This could be both an incentive and disincentive to further study. However, information about the newly introduced student-loan system was not particularly good, and not clearly understood. In addition, it seemed to be unequally applied so that students formerly on benefit became at risk of the burden of large debts.

Students feared debt and were also worried about workloads, if they felt they would have to take on paid work to subsidise further study. References to finances also appear in the section on choice of institution, where students from lower-class backgrounds suggest they would feel out of place in universities that attract wealthy students. Here, however, lack of wealth translated into a lack of confidence and self-esteem or a fear that they would be seen as lower class and discriminated against. Very little comment is made about government policy, but it is clear that the funding system provides a barrier to poorer students taking up the chance of higher education.

IMPORTANCE

This study reports that students were dissatisfied with, and poorly informed about, current funding arrangements for higher education. This is politically significant because it is critical of the very government who funded the research work. It is important because it illustrates in very few pages something about the nature of our society in terms of social policy and planning that, although well known, is still rarely seen to such clear effect. The government states that it wishes to expand lower class participation in education, it sets targets for institutions and yet it still creates policies that are intended to appeal to voters and that actively dissuade the lower classes from applying to universities. This is a case study in social and political incompetence, written in impartial and measured terms, which is supported by both qualitative and quantitative evidence.

EVALUATION

There are few surprises for anyone involved in education in terms of the conclusions and findings of the study. That the education system seems to benefit the higher social classes, possibly at the expense of the lower social classes and the disadvantaged, is a pattern that is so well established that it barely raises an eyebrow! More importantly, this study offers a clue as to some of the processes that occur which have this effect on members of the lower classes at the point of entry to higher education. The problem is slightly less one of culture, as many theorists argue, than one of finance and sheer practicality. Lower-class people are not patronised by the assumption that they do not appreciate the benefits of higher education; rather, they are treated as rational people who fully understand their social situations and who make informed and sensible decisions on that basis.

One of the major strengths of this research is that it is clearly written and is about an interesting and relevant topic for many students. It acts as a model of quantitative research backed up by qualitative understandings – this is triangulation in action. While a small amount of theory is present, the focus of this study is on how people behave and how they make decisions.

In terms of reliability, this study is a remarkable piece of work. A wide range of institutions and students participated in this work. Equally, the study is valid. We learn of the opinions of the respondents, which gives a human dimension to the data. The most interesting results to read are the interview findings, but obviously the evidence has been selected. The quotations offer an insight into individual decision-making processes. However, there is also abundant graphical material which shows through the numerical data provided that the information in the interviews is representative of the views of a wide selection of students.

In addition to the previously mentioned strengths, there is a serious attempt to broaden the scope of this study beyond events in London: this study acknowledges the existence of a world beyond the M25.

QUESTIONS

KNOWLEDGE AND UNDERSTANDING

1. Who commissioned the report? Why?
2. What was the social context of the research?
3. What were the aims of this research?
4. What three samples were used?
5. What four factors influence lower-class students in their decision to participate in higher education?
6. In what ways do lower-class students differ from higher-class students?
7. Explain how considerations of finance can affect a person's decision to participate in higher education.

ANALYSIS

1. What practical problems did the Institute for Employment Studies team face in conducting this study?
2. Outline and explain the significance of the concept of triangulation to sociological study.
3. Evaluate the research under each of the following headings: practicality, reliability, ethics, validity, and representativeness.

RATIONING EDUCATION: POLICY, PRACTICE, REFORM AND EQUITY

David Gillborn and Deborah Youdell

Open University Press, Buckingham, 2000

CONTEXT

Although new, this study is not especially typical of the most recent research produced by sociologists of education as it is concerned with educational inequality and the mechanisms that produce it. Late-1990s educational research often focuses on schools and how improvements can be made to the quality of the service that they offer to students. This is a response to the needs of government funding-agencies that are concerned with improving education. This research, however, was funded by a grant from the Nuffield Foundation. The Nuffield Foundation is an independent charity that funds education and social-welfare projects involved with action or research. (It may be useful to visit their website at www.nuffieldfoundation.org)

The focus of this study is on educational inequality and how it is created. It issues a direct challenge to government press releases about inclusive education and improving standards for all. The claim it makes is simple: schools are places that are active in producing class and ethnic divisions. There is less equality of opportunity in British schools for black and working-class children. Government reforms that are claimed to improve educational standards for all are creating a divisive and unequal system in which the vulnerable are receiving less opportunity for success. These reforms have, to the complaint of teachers, been relentless. Funding systems, examinations, inspections, governance, management styles and curriculum innovation have all been overhauled by a succession of government intercessions by both the Conservatives in the 1980s and then Labour in the late 1990s.

METHODS

Gillborn began his research career in the 1980s in comprehensive schools and this research was intended to repeat some of the methods of that previous work in a second project which took place between autumn 1995 and summer 1997. Specifically, however, it was intended to look at the impact of more recent changes on equality of provision.

The aims of the study were to:

- explore the experience of educational change upon teachers and pupils.
- assess the impact of educational change on equality and achievement among pupils.

Initially the team had access to three schools, two in London and one in the Midlands. Through no fault of the research team, the Midlands school withdrew, however, and this had an impact on the sample. The Midlands school had a high proportion of Asian pupils and so the remaining two schools were mostly composed of white and black (African-Caribbean) pupils. The schools were selected because of certain shared characteristics: they were multi-ethnic and coeducational. They were separated in terms of funding because one was a good comprehensive and the other was a weaker grant-maintained school.

The schools offered the research teams high-status members of staff to act as liaison and gatekeepers. They negotiated differing amounts of access so they had more chance to move about in the comprehensive school, 'Taylor' than in the grant-maintained school, 'Clough'.

- **Taylor School** was a popular school in an outer London borough with a strong commitment to mixed-ability teaching. Pupils were mostly white, but there was a range of other ethnicities present. There was a large proportion of middle-class pupils, including the children of teachers, but a third of the students qualified for free school meals. The school had high levels of attainment and scored well in league tables.
- **Clough School** had no sixth form and a poor local reputation which meant that it found it difficult to attract pupils to fill the available places. It had applied for Grant Maintained status to improve its income. The majority of the pupils were male. They were also white, but there was a high proportion of pupils from minority ethnic groups attending the school. The intake of ability in the school was slewed below average and the school was ranked low in terms of level of achievement.

The researchers used qualitative methods and focused on Year 11 and Year 9 pupils over a two-year period. These groups were chosen so that the team could look at subject choice and study advice for Year 9, and so Year 11 could reflect on their experience of school and expectations. One day a week was spent in each of the study schools over this two-year period and existing tutor groups were used as samples. Teachers were interviewed over a period of time and there were repeat interviews. They focused on English and Maths as being the two most significant subjects and so a succession of lessons was observed, as well as assemblies, parents' evenings and staff meetings. There were informal discussions and observations of tutorial sessions, Personal and Social Education sessions, break times and lunchtimes. Again, access at 'Taylor' was easier than access at 'Clough'.

KEY FINDINGS

The education system of Britain has become obsessed with measurement and with standards so that school economy and performance is geared to raising the number of pupils attaining five A–C passes and improving the school's position in the league tables. This concern started under the Conservative administration after 1979 and has continued through into the Labour administration. There is a very detailed account of legislative change and a concern with the impact of these changes on schools. It is noted that despite the change of language in political discussions from a rhetoric of 'choice' for the Conservatives to a series of public policy statements about 'social justice' under Labour, in practical terms little has changed, so that the market-based educational reforms begun under Margaret Thatcher have become consolidated by Labour. The authors are highly critical of school-effectiveness research on the basis that this ignores social factors that lead to inequality and turns the focus for 'failure' onto schools and teachers. It also criticises the then Chief Inspector of Schools at Ofsted, Chris Woodhead, for misleading, sexist and racialised commentary. The impact of successive government policies has been to widen inequalities of gender, ethnic origin and social class.

Schools have become dominated by a need to appear in a good position in league tables, of which the principle measure of success is the number of pupils achieving five A–C passes. There is a great deal at stake for schools in terms of position in these tables because this can attract parents to send their children to certain schools. Income is generated by pupil numbers. This creates an ethos within schools, to which teachers do not all necessarily subscribe, which the research team call *the A–C economy*. 'Clough' school had decided to go Grant Maintained in the first place to improve the status of the school and to attract more students of higher ability. It perceived itself as having far too many students at the lower end of the ability range as measured by reading tests. A major decision as to the organisation and funding of the school had been made not on political or social grounds but as a response to the demands of the A–C economy. Interestingly, the words 'ability' and 'middle class' tended to merge in meaning in the language of the staff of the school as they discussed intake. Underlying that particular joining of meaning was another slightly more sinister one, which is that 'middle class' and 'white' were also often linked in teacher's minds. This association is furthered by the school's reliance on bought-in tests that appear to predict pupils' progress and potential, but that tend to underplay the ability of minority ethnic and recent-immigrant children at age 11.

The use of tests to predict ability and the pressure to achieve high grades has led some schools to re-introduce/emphasise streaming and banding or to rely on selection of pupils for certain groups. This leads to a focus in schools on those pupils who may attain a large number of the higher grades to improve the results for the school overall. Those perceived as lower ability are encouraged to lower their sights and to choose non-academic or non-examination subjects. This extends into the advice they are given by careers programmes which constantly reinforce the need to aim for five higher-grade passes irrespective of pupils' own ambitions or targets.

Gillborn and Youdell point out that many teachers are very unhappy with the kinds of decisions and policies they are forced to administer and point to the unease many feel with tiered examination papers. They emphasise the fear that teachers have of mis-entering a child for a higher tier, who then gains an unclassified award irrespective of talent or interest in a subject. From a departmental point of view it makes far more sense to enter children for lower tiers where they will gain C grades, irrespective of the impact that this may have on each individual's grade pattern when attempting to enter higher education. This decision process leads schools to having to impose sets, because in some subjects the syllabus is different for the different tiers. Graphs are drawn to shown the correlation between those taking free school meals and those who are non-white, and their entry for tiered examinations in 'Clough'. The pattern is clear. Higher-tier papers and subsequent entry to university is for wealthier white students.

Schools are also pressured into tackling that small group of pupils who are on the borderline between achieving five A–Cs and failing to gain that target. Already teachers focus on those who will improve the A–C rate for the whole school by gaining far more than five passes, but now the borderliners are brought into policy planning. This leaves those who are not entered or predicted to fail in a position of increasing inequality of provision and attention. Curiously, the initiatives to target the middle band were not particularly successful in raising standards in that group in Taylor school. Pupils themselves had only a hazy understanding of what underlies some of the decisions made about them by teachers but the impact on them was that those in lower sets tended to have a sense of disaffection and disassociation from the process. They experience confusion and, in some cases, despair.

IMPORTANCE This study shows the essential need for researchers to look at the macro level and understand the social structures such as government policy that impose certain limitations on social process; there is also the need to look at the micro level and see what impact issues have on social interaction.

There is, however, a wider argument here, too. Constant small-scale niggling racism may provoke a reaction so that large numbers of black boys are frequently excluded from schools. However, by throwing the focus onto the child and the individual school, the government is shelving its obligation to do something about the deep-seated and institutional inequalities and racism of British society.

EVALUATION

This book offers a refreshing counterpoint to much recent educational research in that its aims are radical and critical of government. It is realistic, honest and deeply analytical in its appraisal of what the implications of government policy are for those who have to implement it and for those who are, in fact, the subject of it: the pupils.

It is a measured account which offers understanding of all of the participants in the educational process. Teachers are uneasy and unhappy about decision-making processes and using testing strategies that in some cases they find dubious, but which they have little choice but to accept, and pupils are embarrassed and degraded by the pressure of the tactics that schools sometimes misguidedly apply to raise their own position in league tables. Racism and class discrimination feature in the schools, but it is subtle and associated with assumed measures of ability. Pupils find it hard to actually pinpoint cases of bias, but they know that they have been short-changed by the education system.

This book should be compulsory reading for those concerned with making policy decisions. It is not a quick read for a student, but it is fairly straightforward because it is not sociology that is written for other sociologists, but sociology that describes and explains the daily processes by which people frame their lives. It points out how government policy and rhetoric about increasing standards and success hides an increasingly unfair and unequal system by focusing on standards and ignoring those who are likely to fail or be failed by the system.

QUESTIONS

KNOWLEDGE AND UNDERSTANDING

1. Who commissioned the report?
2. What was the social context of the research?
3. What were the aims of this research?
4. Describe the sampling process used in the study.
5. What is the 'A–C economy' and how does it operate?
6. Why do black students and working-class students find it difficult to pinpoint bias and discrimination in their treatment by schools?
7. How are teachers and students failed by the system of tiering GCSE examinations?
8. Why do Gillborn and Youdell reject recent sociological research into school effectiveness?

ANALYSIS

1. Why is it necessary for sociologists to use both micro and macro approaches to any research study if they wish to have an overview of a social interaction.
2. Evaluate the work of the Gillborn and Youdell under each of the following headings: practicality, reliability, ethics, validity, and representativeness.

MARKETS, CHOICE AND EQUITY IN EDUCATION

Sharon Gewirtz, Stephen J Ball, Richard Bowe

Open University Press, Buckingham, 1995

CONTEXT

This book reflects the newer thrust of educational research that developed in the 1980s and 1990s as a result of the massive changes brought about by the 1979–97 Conservative government's reforms to the education system. From concerns with the running and daily interaction of schools typical of the 1970s and 1980s, research began to focus more precisely on the organisational and structural factors that make a school effective and popular with parents. Partly this was a reaction to the changes, which were not completely popular with educationalists (who saw the market-based policies as being socially divisive), but there was also a political drive for academics to produce 'useful' work that could comment on and influence policy decisions. This was dictated by the need for researchers to obtain funding for their work.

The social and political theories of the New Right were concerned with introducing market forces into public services in order to improve efficiency and prevent wastage of money. There was an ideological flavour to the debate because the New Right felt that the introduction of competition into daily life provided a more individual service in comparison with the governmentally organised services that had been a legacy of welfare provision since 1945. Hospitals, GPs, social services, prison services, transport provision, telecommunications, housing provision, community care and dental care were all being privatised and made subject to market forces at the same time. A variety of researchers have noted that in each case, although the principle of market was applied the actual systems and results were very different. This book is concerned with the impact of concepts of 'market' to education systems and on schools in particular.

The research team for this study contend that an 'education market' does not exist as such because of the complexity of local authorities and local provision. However, they do claim to be able to discern trends and patterns brought about by the introduction of competition between schools to attract parents as consumers. They are critical of earlier research in the field because they claim that much work into parental choice views parents as being logical and informed consumers. This, they argue, ignores the complexity of human factors and the general messiness of the choice process. They are concerned, too, with school and Local Education Authority processes. Much of the current research that they were responding to focused on either the impact of changes on LEA and school-management systems or on whether there was any reality to the choice that policy, in theory, was supposed to offer. Finally, they chose to investigate the impact of the previous two elements of the debate on the actual provision of schooling.

METHODS

The study was conducted between 1991 and 1994. Data was collected from three London boroughs that were geographically linked in terms of being close to each other, but which were very different in terms of social and ethnic mix. The team was particularly interested in secondary-education provision because this was the area where market choice has most impact on the quality of provision. Thirteen schools were studied and these were given false names to conceal their identities. The names were chosen with some degree of humour: 'Pankhurst' for a girl's school and 'Flightpath' for another. (One can only speculate that 'Trumpton' was named in honour of a child's television programme notable for wooden puppets!)

The authors were concerned to look at the effect of market forces on schools with respect to:

- parental choice
- school responses
- the outcome of market forces on the distribution and quality of provision.

To understand the Local Education Authorities, the authors attended meetings, used LEA data on parental choice and school performance indicators, and also read official minutes, plans and documents.

They conducted interviews with parents of primary-age pupils. The process of contacting parents was scientifically rigorous, insofar as it was possible, in order to ensure that the samples reflected the population distributions of the various boroughs. The first two years of sampling were opportunistic but the third year of interviews was based on the researchers seeking groups who were under-represented and targeting them. Interviews were conducted at the time that the parents were involved in the process of selecting a school for their children. Interviews lasted for between half an hour to two hours. 119 interviews were also conducted with a range of other interested people: Headteachers of primary schools, secondary Heads, Deputy Heads, Chairs of Governors and a range of staff, including some of whom filled more than one role, but who were only counted as single interviews. Again, they collected a range of secondary data such as school policies, brochures and minutes of meetings. Gradually, they narrowed their focus onto a range of what they considered to be 'theoretically interesting schools'.

KEY FINDINGS

PARENTS IN THE MARKETPLACE

The aim of introducing market forces into education was justified by the government in two ways: as an extension of personal freedom and also to improve schools as they compete to attract parents – who are effectively 'customers' for education. Publications by the Department of Education in the early 1990s reflected these viewpoints by using a 'language of choice'. Consumerism was supported by publication in newspaper and book-form of lists of 'Good State Schools' and school league tables of results. Critics of the consumer-based approach pointed to the impact of the social-class entry of schools on results so that effective schools in poorer areas appeared to be doing less well than poorly led schools in wealthy areas. The researchers have used the concept of cultural capital as described by Bourdieu to identify parents as belonging to categories of choice-making:

- **Privileged/skilled choosers** were generally middle class and often orientated to élite and competitive schools. These parents arrange for their children to attend the correct primaries and then use negotiating skills and training of their children to ensure that they are accepted by the selected schools. They attempt to match the ethos of the school to the nature of the child using a sense of the school ethos, and also referring to pupil behaviours, sometimes in overtly class-laden tones.
- **Semi-skilled choosers**, mixed-class group of aspirant working-class parents. They were highly motivated for their children, but were less aware of some of the social

nuance and insider knowledge of the system necessary in order to privilege their children. They were more open to media reports of the schools or they relied on the judgements of others. Many did not fully understand the significance and meanings of the open evenings and brochures and so they relied on reputation and rumour in their selection processes. They also commented on the ethnic mix of schools in mildly racist terms.
- **Disconnected choosers**, who were less able to make choices, often viewed parental choice as being of little significance and viewed all schools as 'being much the same'. They usually made their selections on geography or on the current 'happiness' of the child rather than in terms of job prospects or the personality and nature of the child.

The research team points out the dangers of taking these categories too seriously or linking them too closely to the class structure which is itself in a state of flux. They simply suggest these as ideal types against which to measure the ways that choice is made. The significant factor for them is that school choices are social choices, based on culture and group and that not all parents are equally equipped in terms of knowledge or decision-making skills.

LOCAL MARKET RELATIONS

The main findings here are that LEAs have some degree of control over their local markets, and that relationships between local education authorities and the schools they exist to serve are complex and sometimes very unfriendly.

SCHOOL ORGANISATIONS

This chapter focuses on the role of the Headteacher, though it acknowledges the significance of governing bodies. This is a role that was enhanced during the Conservative governments of the 1980s and early 1990s. Heads were given more control over their own finances and could increase their income by attracting pupils. The concomitant is that if schools are unpopular, they lose money! In schools whose catchment is composed of working-class children from deprived estates, there is the very real possibility of staff redundancy and school closure. This has imposed a new managerial role on headteachers, who previously were seen in an academic and curriculum role. Senior management teams have to galvanise staff to 'sell' schools to pupils and parents but also to accept redundancies, too, if school rolls fall. This has led to a whole raft of initiatives and a dramatic culture change that encourages heads to think in terms of corporate image, vision and organisational structures and to impose these elements of thinking onto their institutions. Many headteachers were uncomfortable with this new role, sometimes because of philosophical beliefs in comprehensives, or because it conflicted with their older values of teacher professionalism. Tensions also emerged as heads were forced to embrace new ways of thinking but were not communicating their changing philosophies to staff. The research team point to power struggles between staff and senior management teams who misunderstand each other's motivation.

SCHOOLS IN THE NEW MARKETPLACE

Schools need to create an 'image' that is attractive to parents and students. They do this through school policy, documentation, the building, management style, name and their students. Newly developed schools needed to create instant 'traditions' through logos and uniforms. Senior members of staff were dedicated to marketing schools particularly in those schools that had cause to fear falling pupil numbers because of their intake or social geography. There were significant refurbishment schemes taking place and money was spend on liaising with the press or opening the schools on a variety of evenings. Most of the schools had new reception areas with a 'business-like feel'. School documentation had to fit in with a 'school style'.

Individualism was becoming a thing of the past and conservatism in dress emphasised values of hard work and strong discipline. School prospectuses were better produced and glossy, but less informative; one school had bought in the services of an advertising agency. The concern was to give schools a more middle-class flavour in order to attract the high-achieving child of ambitious parents. The term 'able' had, in certain contexts, become code for 'middle class'. Interestingly, schools were anxious to attract females in particular because they are seen as being more responsive to discipline and producing better results. Musical ability was seen as a form of social selector for middle-class and concerned parents, so choirs and dance groups were encouraged. South Asian (presumably Hindu or Indian background) children were attractive to schools.

Unattractive intakes consisted of less able, emotionally damaged children with learning disabilities. Ability, again, is used as a code for social class, with low-ability and working-class backgrounds being used in a connective sense. Integration was resisted for children with Special Educational Needs in some schools, not for sound educational reasons, but because of the possible perceptions of parents. There was only implicit evidence, but the researchers do point out that African-Caribbean boys may well be the victims of covert de-selection. The significance of all of this is that image-making is turning schools into organisations that value certain children above others. The market does not ensure equality of access for all, if schools only desire the custom of certain groups at the expense of others. There is an uneasy balance for schools who wish to promote values of equality and anti-racism at the same time as attracting the 'correct' students who are middle class, musical, female and white or Indian.

INSIDE SCHOOLS

The impact of market forces on the internal practice of schools has already been discussed in terms of managerial cultural change. However, a number of other areas are affected. Policy-makers in schools tend to use short-term and superficial strategies to solve problems that require deep-seated and radical solutions. Instant policies include concerns with uniform – uniforms market schools well because they foster an impression of discipline, but harshly enforced uniform rules disrupt teacher–pupil relationships and may provoke truancy. Schools are responding to truancy problems rather than addressing the causes of discontent. The team report on unofficial or 'constructive exclusions' where schools 'recommend' that social undesirables may wish to look for another school. Problem children can then be shunted around the education system without anyone addressing the issue of the causes of poor behaviour. Socially exclusive practices such as creating complex application forms that require high levels of literacy ensure that only the more 'able' parents apply; this is a form of covert racism since forms are frequently only available in English. There are particular concerns over provision for children with Special Educational Needs who are expensive to teach, but who do not gain the examination grades necessary to prove that schools are performing effectively.

The findings can be summarised as follows.

- The market, as a system for organising a social structure, benefits the middle class.
- Parental choices of schools are made on class and 'race' grounds.
- Schools are responding by meeting the needs of middle-class parents and appealing to their perceptions.
- Schools are becoming increasingly unequal and are losing their commitment to the comprehensive ideal of 'each according to need'.

IMPORTANCE

All the indications are that there will be increasing moves to offer greater parental choice under New Labour. They have not reversed New-Right policies, but endorsed them. Recently (2001), the Education White Paper has suggested that there will be more faith schools, which will be funded and supported through religious groupings. The current Prime Minister has expressed great support for individualised schools that will support the needs of all parents. This is very controversial, especially in the light of the risk of ethnic and religious disharmony as a result of the terrorist acts that destroyed the World Trade Centre (2001) and of the subsequent reactions of Western governments. In the light of government reluctance to address issues of inequality in British society, and New Labour's regard for the workings of market, this book should gain significance and importance as a guide for future social-policy research.

EVALUATION

This book is a stunning indictment of the impact of market forces on education for the deprived and less-educated sectors of the community. It uses a tightly argued and methodologically sound base for arguing that schools are contributing to a deep and widening inequality of British society, regardless of their professional and ideological aims of equality and care. It asks some fundamental questions as to the extent to which parents are discerning consumers educated to understand the systems into which they are buying. Clearly, many are not – and so the middle classes are able to use their cultural capital to ensure privilege for their children. On the other hand, the values of community and the economics of poverty ensure that however much working-class parents value their children and wish to support them, they will be excluded by market forces that deem their off-spring an undesirable educational commodity. An underlying theme of the text is that inequalities are not just issues of class, but of race and to a lesser extent, gender. We are increasingly a segregated society.

QUESTIONS

KNOWLEDGE AND UNDERSTANDING

1. How many local authorities did the research team study?
2. Who was interviewed in the course of the research?
3. What were the aims of this research?
4. What are 'market forces'?
5. Identify two sources of secondary data used.
6. Why did schools try to develop a corporate image?
7. How do schools use the concept of educational ability to be socially divisive?

ANALYSIS

1. How reliable is this study? Refer to the variety of techniques and how they were used.
2. To what extent do market forces ensure equality of provision and responsiveness of schools to the needs of all parents?
3. What do you consider to be the chief policy implications of this study for schools and for government?

DIVIDE AND SCHOOL:
GENDER AND CLASS DYNAMICS IN A COMPREHENSIVE SCHOOL

John Abraham

Falmer Press, London, 1995

CONTEXT

This book reports on an ethnographic study of a comprehensive school referred to as Greenfield Comprehensive. The fieldwork was conducted in 1986. Its focus was to examine how social class and gender divisions are reinforced by the school and how the school reproduces social differences.

Abraham believes Greenfield to be a good school. Staff did not deliberately attempt to discriminate. Unlike some early ethnographic research into schools, this is not an attempt to suggest that teachers carry the responsibility for the failure of schools to provide equality of access. In fact, Abraham tends to support the concept of comprehensive schooling and to be critical of what was then current government thinking, which aimed to reform and challenge comprehensive schools. A rather broader set of aims is to understand the complex sets of relationships that exist in schools.

Abraham conducted his research at a time when the pace of government changes in school was very rapid. The radical reforms of the Conservative government's Education Reform Acts (ERA 1986 and 1988) were yet to be fully implemented in the education system, but schools were aware of the implications. Curiously, Abraham was taking a critical look at the implementation of the equality aims of comprehensive schools just as this idea was finally going out of fashion among policy-makers – who were talking in terms of 'excellence' and 'competition'.

Abraham's own position is made clear in the introduction. He feels that it is important to reduce class and gender divisions in society and that schools can be part of the process of changing society. Note that while all schools currently (2002) have gender- and ethnic-equality policies, there is significantly less commitment at any level of the political or educational system to the reduction of class inequality in British schools.

Abraham looked for examples of:

- **Differentiation**: the ranking of children according to the values of the school
- **Polarisation**: the division of children according to their own acceptance of the values of the school. He saw them as forming opposing groups, supporting or disaffected from the school.

METHODS

Abraham chose to produce a detailed study of a single school because he wished to explore social processes in depth.

The school studied:

- was mixed sex
- had a wide range of academic ability and social class in its intake
- streamed children into subject sets according to their perceived abilities in that subject alone

- covered a wide geographical area with a range of housing types
- was regarded by the local population as having a good academic reputation
- had very few minority ethnic pupils
- was strict in applying rules about uniforms.

The reason for this choice was that the school fitted the profile of one in which gender and social class could be easily studied without a variety of other variables intruding on the results.

The study group was the 300 pupils in what would now be known as Year 10, but which were then referred to as Year 4; they were 14–15 years old. The age-group choice was made because the students could opt for subjects and because they had some prior records and history in the school that could be used for the purposes of comparisons and experience. The focus of the study was on a sample drawn from sets at various ability levels in English, Maths and French, which comprised just under half of the year group. Note the absence of science sets from the more detailed study – the reason for this is partly historical because the National Curriculum, with its emphasis on Science as a core subject, had not then been introduced.

The techniques used both qualitative and quantitative methods, including:

- observations – some of them participant, and many of them based on pre-formatted observation schedules
- pupil questionnaires that included information on friendships, career prospects, subject choice and the questionnaire itself
- unstructured interviewing of teachers and pupils
- sampling of textbooks and student's notes.

KEY FINDINGS

Although this is basically an ethnographic study and therefore concerned with emotions, meaning and process, it also uses a considerable amount of supporting quantitative data gathered through the observations. Abraham relied on school records, for instance, to discover social class, and correlates these with scores relating to academic achievement.

ORGANISATIONAL DIFFERENCES

- *Teachers* – Abraham found support for labelling theories and notes that the behaviours in top sets were seen as being better by the teachers. Few top-set children experienced serious sanctions, whereas lower-set children were far more often likely to be removed from lessons or reported for bad behaviour. More significantly, working-class pupils tended to be found in lower sets. Sets, in Abraham's view, worked against the egalitarian principles of the comprehensive system.
- *Pupils* – Children often form friendship groupings with other pupils who share the same values, so pro-school and anti-school friendship groups develop. Pro-school friendship groups tend to form in the upper sets and the lower sets form anti-school groups. Friendship groups tended to form within genders. Anti-school girls tended to be more tolerant of pro-school friendship groups, in contrast to the boys where there was some intolerance.

DEVIANCE

- *Class* – Lower sets tend to be more unruly than higher sets. This is a pattern that develops within the school as setting becomes more significant in the older classes.
- *Gender* – Teachers complained that boys generate problems of ill-discipline and poor behaviour. In fact, boys were told off more than girls. Abraham offers two possible theories to account for this, and both refer to teacher expectations – even though he goes on to discuss the ways that boys dominate and control classroom interactions through unruliness. He notes that many girls complain of lack of

attention from teachers or complain about the system operated by the school. It was the anti-school groups of both genders who followed the stereotypical gender patterns to the highest degree; so anti-school girls wore make-up and took gendered subjects such as Typing and Home Economics whereas anti-school boys had stereotypical views of females based on sexuality rather than relationships.

SUBJECT OPTIONS

- *Class* – Students in lower-ability sets were likely to opt for 'new' subjects at GCE and CSE (later to become GCSE) whereas those in upper sets tend to choose along traditional lines. This had implications for students from working-class backgrounds who were often guided towards practical subjects with more liberal teachers. Traditional 'academic' subjects had good academic results and cohorts of middle-class students entering their subjects.
- *Gender* – Interestingly, many middle-class girls showed a tendency to opt for traditional male subjects and to relate these choices to future career aspirations, but very few males chose to study subject areas they considered feminine. Peer and parental pressure tended to be conservative and to push students towards traditional subject-choice patterns.

KNOWLEDGE

- *Class* – Knowledge was selected for pupils by teachers and so lower-set students were not given certain topics to study for fear of their responses. This was seen as particularly relevant to issues of challenging gender assumptions by teachers. To a certain extent knowledge is defined by the demands of the examination boards. Achievement tended to be related not so much to ability as to the effort made by the students.
- *Gender* – Textbooks, and teacher interpretations of them, tended to be implicitly and sometimes explicitly gendered. Boys would often attempt to bully girls out of taking subjects that they felt belonged to the male domain, but the school intervened to support the girls in such situations.

TEACHER IDEOLOGY

Abraham did not find that teachers shared a political ideology. Some were explicitly in favour of gender equality, whereas one explicitly rejected it. Class is not mentioned in this section of the work.

OVERALL RECOMMENDATIONS

- Reduce streaming even though this may have an impact on results.
- Reduce competitiveness in teaching and examination strategy.
- Reduce sex-stereotyping by allowing pupils more choice of identity; for instance, by abandoning school uniform.
- Control GCSE/CSE choices options to diminish class and gendering of subjects.
- Train teachers into class and gender understandings.
- Clear anti-sexist policies should exist in schools.
- Reflective curriculum to reinforce the comprehensive ideal.

IMPORTANCE This study is both personal and institutional in its scope and many of its findings and recommendations have been superseded by new concerns and educational debates prompted by the reforming legislation of the late 1980s and 1990s. Its significance is that it looks at the institution in terms of comparing aims with the means used to attain those objectives and thus identifies areas of tension. It moves from a concern with pupils to seeing teachers and institutions as being part of the process of transmitting culture and is more sympathetic to teachers than many similar works. It makes an early, considered, head-on and ultimately futile attack on the provisions of the Educational Reform Acts of 1986 and 1988.

EVALUATION

Even though this work is relatively recent in publication, many of the cultural references to fashions, attitudes and current events seem curiously dated because this work was conducted over 15 years ago. Equally some of the school structures and activities described are no longer possible due to the impact of the National Curriculum on the running and organisation of schools. Thinking has moved very quickly on issues of gender in schools, whereas class is increasingly overlooked. There is rather less discussion offered on issues of class in the text than perhaps there should be as 'lower sets' and 'working class' seem to be assumed to mean almost the same thing in most of the work. This does not do justice to the complexity of issues of class in modern Britain, particularly as widening gaps in equality and poverty were beginning to make themselves felt over much of Britain.

Class and gender tend to be treated as separate topics throughout the text, but the evidence and discussion suggest that class and gender are more significantly linked than Abraham takes account of. For instance, he notes that upper-set girls challenge masculinities in relation to subject choices and working-class girls do not. However, this does not lead to a separate discussion of the differences between these two groups of girls or in the social differences between working-class and middle-class boys who actually seem to share cultural values that are marginally closer than those of the two disparate groups of girls.

Importantly, Science still tends to be a gendered and masculine subject area and its absence as a study subject in favour of French is curious in the light of this study's aims. There is little emphasis on it, except in the student responses – in which a long discussion about it takes place. This area seems to have been a little under-researched, especially in the light of the fact that new technology and computers were already being introduced into schools in the 1980s.

Quotations tend to be taken from the dramatic and exciting students who form anti-school groups so while we know little about the conformists, the rebellious are made to seem heroic. However, this study is far less guilty of celebrating the non-academic than many in the genre. It is clear the sympathies of the author lie with the students. He allows the students to talk of the teachers 'who can't control the class'.

Abraham is sometimes a little patronising in his views of the teachers, accusing one of having 'a shaky assumption' when she refers to her own experiences. Some of the teachers have over 19 years' experience in education; it is possible that they are using experiential and pragmatic knowledge which, while not in line with Abraham's observations and theoretical understandings, works for them. In places, one senses that the teachers may even be having a little fun at Abraham's expense!

QUESTIONS

KNOWLEDGE AND UNDERSTANDING

1 Describe the characteristics of the school Abraham studied.
2 What did Abraham's main study group consist of?
3 What were the aims of this research?
4 What was the relationship between achievement and ability?
5 Identify two different methods used.
6 Which gender and class were more able to challenge traditional patterns?
7 To what extent did the school as an organisation contribute to or reinforce traditional gender and class patterns?
8 What recommendations did Abraham make for implementing increasing equality in comprehensive schools?

ANALYSIS

1 What practical and ethical problems might Abraham have faced in conducting this study?
2 To what extent can the findings of Abraham be considered to be relevant to schools in the early 2000s?
3 Evaluate the work of Abraham under each of the following headings: practicality, reliability, ethics, validity, and representativeness.

BLACK MASCULINITIES AND SCHOOLING:
HOW BLACK BOYS SURVIVE MODERN SCHOOLING

Tony Sewell

Trentham Books, Stoke-on-Trent, 1997

CONTEXT

Much of the early research on relationships between education and gender was carried out by feminists who were researching reasons for female underachievement. However, the conclusions of this early research were made redundant by the mid-1980s when it appeared that a different pattern of school achievement was emerging. Both boys and girls were gaining better examination results, but girls were tending to achieve higher results than boys. This pattern was misinterpreted as a 'failure' among boys and became something of a moral panic. Feminists and others became interested in masculinities.

There is a further dimension to this debate, however, which is that the relative underachievement of boys of African-Caribbean descent had been widely documented since the 1970s. Black boys were significantly over-represented among those who went to Special Schools specifically for those with learning and behavioural difficulties. The Swann Report of 1985 suggested that some of the reasons for this lie within African-Caribbean culture. Sewell deliberately set out to reject this cultural thesis and to seek alternative accounts of the failure of African-Caribbean students which lie within the shared meanings of the school and the boys themselves as to the nature of 'race' and 'sexuality'.

Note that throughout this work, Sewell uses the term 'black' to describe boys of African-Caribbean origin. At the time of this study, Sewell was in his early thirties, and defines himself as 'black'.

METHODS

The study used very informal methods of data collection but is supported by reference to a wide range of secondary materials such as exclusion figures for Inner London and literary references to black writers such as James Baldwin. Sewell gathered his material 'through semi-structured interviews and observations'. He made detailed notes at the end of each day. He also spent time observing classrooms. He is careful to point out that he was able to make very good relationships with the boys and was able to mix with them socially. He describes this process as being able to 'chill'. Because he felt there was a danger of over-identifying with his study group, he used a method he described as 'emancipatory' which involved returning to people and re-interviewing them. This process of double interviewing allowed respondents time to reflect and comment on his work.

The aims of the study were to look at:

- how the school acts as an agency for the sexual and racial oppression of African-Caribbean boys
- how the boys respond to the oppression in order to create their own meanings and to survive.

The pilot study was conducted in what Sewell called 'John Caxton School'. This first school had 700 students and was mixed sex, though predominantly male in intake and consisted of '30% white, 30% Afro-Caribbean and 30% Asian'. These bland figures probably mask a school with a very variable ethnic mix. However, one figure is very significant: of these students, 85% of the total exclusions were of African-Caribbean boys. Sewell's discussion focuses on interviews with two teachers, one black male and one white female. Both of these teachers are professed left-wing liberals who identify racism within the school and point to cultural difficulties that exist with the black boys. Within this context Sewell suggests that teachers are socialised by the act of teaching to defend the dominant racist ethos of the school even if they appear to personally attempt to challenge it. He altered the terms of his original thesis to include new themes including 'teacher socialisation' and a political theme of 'teacher legitimacy'.

The bulk of the study was conducted in 'Township School'. This school was a boys comprehensive for children aged 11–16. There were '61 students of Asian origin, 63 of African origin, 140 of African-Caribbean origin, 31 mixed race students, 127 white boys and 23 others'. The school was located in a wealthy area, but a large number of public schools in the area catered for middle-class children. This school had a high proportion of free dinners, and there was evidence of other forms of social deprivation among the intake. Few of the boys at the school came from the local region, they travelled from inner-city areas to the school. The newly appointed Headteacher was black and a recent (1994) Ofsted report of the school was damning. Exclusion figures pointed to a very tense relationship between the African-Caribbean boys and the 30 teachers on the staff.

KEY FINDINGS

After initial contact, Sewell created three categories of teacher.

1 **Supportive teachers** accounted for 10% of the staff and aimed to be mentors to the students. These were the teachers best able to make good relationships with difficult students.
2 **Irritated teachers** were the largest category and consisted of 60% of the staff. They blamed the subculture of the boys for their antagonism to the school and felt that the problems of the school were caused by indiscipline. Sewell later allocates the notion 'ambivalent' to teachers in this category who showed that they were both supportive and antagonistic towards elements of black culture.
3 **Antagonistic teachers** were either overtly racist or disliked expressions of African-Caribbean culture.

Sewell's analysis claims that many teachers are frightened of the black boys in school. He suggests that the culture of the school and the socialisation of teachers into stereotypical assumptions create the problems that the boys experience. He points to the boys' physical size and their sexuality. However, he does note in passing that the low personal morale of the teachers makes them unwilling to tackle the serious issues of the school. The school was in budget deficit, their jobs were threatened and their lack of motivation expressed itself in terms of poor lesson preparation and the use of worksheets to minimise interaction with the students in lessons.

Student responses to the school tend to fall into four typologies, which Sewell borrows from Merton's classic analysis of deviance.

1 **Conformists**, who were said to be adopting white values at the expense of losing their African-Caribbean identities. These were the largest group, but were still less than half the cohort.
2 **Innovators**, who accepted the goals of the school but maintained a rebellious and anti-school posture and were able to avoid trouble through the exercise of intelligent strategies. They remained on the fringes of the rebel group.

3. **Retreatists** were a small group and consisted of the loners who opted out of much social contact.
4. **Rebels** adopted the signs and signals of aggressive African-Caribbean masculinity and rejected the school. Their behaviour was aggressively masculine and they perceived masculinity in terms of sex and money. Their favoured term of abuse was 'pussy' which they used to imply homosexuality or femininity and low status. They were confrontational, even to the extent of smoking cannabis on school premises, and sometimes violent. Other students perceived them to be bullying. The most rebellious group termed themselves the 'posse'.

To summarise, black students were disciplined excessively by teachers who were socialised into racist attitudes and scared of these students' masculinity, sexuality and physical skills. The black boys responded in ways that reinforced those stereotyped views and behaved in ways that could be interpreted as violent and disruptive.

IMPORTANCE This study is fascinating. The ethnographic data and the portrait it paints of a school and a culture in crisis is vivid and exciting. Sewell's ability to understand and explain the meanings of the values and behaviour of the boys he studies is exemplary though his interpretations are decidedly value-laden. Interestingly, Sewell has recently been attacked by many in the black community for suggesting that black culture and peer pressure are as dangerous to the achievement of black children as racism. His recent claim is that an anti-intellectual culture and their control over sport and popular music gives black children status in the eyes of white students but harms their own chances of succeeding through education. His own research in this book has been used by attackers such as Lee Jasper (2002) to claim instead that white female teachers are to blame for the failure of black boys because they are intimidated by them and that their expectations of the boys' behaviour dictates the form and style of the teaching that they offer.

EVALUATION

Throughout the study, Sewell refers to the pupils of African-Caribbean origin as 'black'. This is a troublesome term in sociology because of the racist connotations of what is now seen as negative labelling. It is also awkward because it does not carry the full sense of the wide ethnic mix that may contribute to the African-Caribbean identity. Sewell is therefore signalling his own cultural identification with the boys by using this term in such a way.

It is notable that although there are acknowledgements made to the teachers of Township school, the dedication of the study is to the boys. Sewell's identification with their culture and value system is so strong as to make his final analysis of their relationship with the school decidedly biased in their favour. This does not mean that the picture he paints of a demoralised and failing school is not valid, but there is little discussion of the organisation and structure of that school. The feelings of the Asian or the white boys are rarely discussed and the conformist groups' responses to the anti-school groups are under-represented.

It seems that the teachers in both schools studied are perceived as racist; regardless of politics, stated values, experiences with the students or their own ethnic backgrounds. There is little consideration of their attempts to deal with life in Township, which is clearly a difficult school as seen from their perspective. One woman reports having had her nose broken by a boy and another young woman is regularly called 'white bitch' by classes but these incidents pass without serious comment from Sewell; the implication being that the bullying attacks were justified by the racism of the teachers and their unwillingness to challenge the school system. One student, named as Victor, a dominant gang leader, complains that his teachers consider him aggressive. He remarks of his relationship with a female Asian teacher: 'she would say I'm aggressive when I shout' '... because she's small and I'm big she thinks I'm going to harm her' 'She thinks because I clench my fist that I am about to hit her ...'. Sewell's final approving conclusion is that Victor's behaviour is the rejection of white middle-class ownership of mental activity. Sewell refers to the teacher as 'antagonistic' despite the fact she is a small woman working alone with large classes of unresponsive and physically challenging males in a school where violence against women is not uncommon.

Sewell spends some considerable time discussing the sculpted black hairstyles fashionable and popular with the black students of the 1980s. These were banned by the school. Few of the teachers supported the ban, but nevertheless they were required to implement the policy. This forced them into confrontation with the students and is a clear but under-discussed element of the institutional racism of the school. However, the political and social organisation of the school as an institution is simply not regarded as being significant by Sewell; the focus of the study is so clearly at the interpersonal level. This point is made by Caroline wa Kamau (2000) who says that Sewell examines culture and behaviour without taking into account the context in which it occurs.

Sewell reports shocking behaviour from the teaching staff including abusing pupils out of their hearing, negative stereotyping of their home backgrounds and gross insensitivity. Clearly, the boys do experience racism from the school. Whether this is intentional or a result of cultural misunderstanding remains a moot point given that no teacher in Township school meets Sewell's standards, with the exception of a Mr Howard, himself black, whose perspective 'had its limitations' and who was disliked by other members of staff for his accusatory manner with regard to race issues.

While the insight that Sewell offers into the origins and development of Afro-Caribbean culture and the values of the disaffected are valuable and useful, it is the comments of the respondents themselves that tell us most about the processes of the school. One can note that the accusations of racism directed at the teachers may well be fully justified, but the disaffected youths Sewell studied are not the only victims of the social processes he describes.

QUESTIONS

KNOWLEDGE AND UNDERSTANDING

1. What findings did the Swann Report offer on the relative under-achievement of black boys?
2. What does Sewell mean by 'emancipatory research'?
3. What were the aims of this research?
4. How many schools did Sewell study?
5. What particular fact suggested his claim that schools had tense relationships with their African-Caribbean students?
6. Describe Township school.
7. What categories do teachers tend to fall into in their responses to black students?
8. What categories do students fall into in their responses to the school?

ANALYSIS

1. What problems in using ethnographic research methods does this study illustrate?
2. How valid or reliable do you consider Sewell's work to be?

References Caroline wa Kamau (2000) website: 'The Black World Today'
Jasper, L (2002) 'School system failing black children' in The Guardian, 16 March
Merton, R (1968) *Social Theory and Social Structure*, The Free Press, New York
Swann, Lord (1985), *Education For All*, HMSO, London

IMPROVING SCHOOL EFFECTIVENESS

John MacBeath and Peter Mortimore (eds)

Open University Press, Buckingham, 2001

CONTEXT

This book reports on the Improving School Effectiveness project (ISEP) that began in Scotland in 1994. The project was a response to broad political and educational drives to improve the quality of education in Britain. Its focus is on Scotland but the themes of the research are far broader in scope than just one country and most of the extensive research team have experience of education systems within a variety of different countries.

The editors point out that governments throughout the world have been funding projects about the effectiveness of schools for over thirty years, but that, despite the volume of data gathered, it is still not clear what makes some schools more effective than others.

The authors state categorically that schools can make a difference to the individual life chances of children. However, they underline the point that since schools are not independent of the societies and cultures of which they a part there is no simple answer to the question of how to make schools effective. The issue is to support schools in strategies that are successful and to enable them to become more self-critical so that further development is possible.

There is an enormous international literature on school effectiveness, much of which arises out of social concerns with inequality and the wastage of talent among lower-class and deprived students in the 1960s and 1970s. It is clear that some schools are more effective than others when it comes to enabling children from less-privileged backgrounds to succeed. One of the problems with international research, however, is that there is no universal measure of what effectiveness means. Cultural factors such as the status of teaching as an occupation or the value placed on educational achievement may have an impact on the effectiveness of the educational system. Measures of success vary between education systems and even within schools. Furthermore, schools are not equally effective as institutions. Departments vary in quality. Some schools may offer strong support to students of borderline ability and others are particularly good for one gender or one ethnic grouping.

METHODS

The study demonstrates that quantitative and qualitative methodologies are not necessarily in opposition despite the fact they are drawn from different theoretical understandings. One approach can support the insights gained by the other. In this study the researchers used quantitative methods to gather statistical evidence of school effectiveness, and then ethnographic techniques to understand the processes that occur within schools to make them more or less effective.

The aims of the study were twofold:

- 'to create a valid way of judging the performance of schools taking into account their different intakes'

- 'to gain an understanding of the processes that take place in different types of schools'.

The initial sample of schools was large. 200 schools were contacted and 82 responded. Two schools dropped out of the project, so the survey was of 80 Scottish schools. The balance was slightly in favour of primary schools, with 44 participating. Within the schools, age cohorts (groups) were also selected: 8–9-year-olds and 13–14-year-olds. The sampling therefore consisted of 'some 7,000 pupils in all, plus 2,500 teachers and 5,400 parents' for the first phase of the study. A second phase of the study consisted of 24 case-study schools drawn from the initial sample.

To investigate school effectiveness, it was necessary to learn something of the pupils and the schools themselves. The research team chose ten social and educational factors that could be used as a base for investigating school effectiveness. These were: age, gender, socio-economic factors and earlier measures of school experience. School characteristics including ratio of free school meals and attendance data were used to put pupil progress in context. Students were tested for reading, writing and mathematical attainment over two years. Judgements could be made on the effectiveness of the schools based on the progress of the pupils over the two-year period.

The authors describe their techniques as 'eclectic'. This means that a variety of further methods were used to support the statistical data. These included the following.

- Pupil questionnaires which tested attitudes, self-concept and motivation. This was an important part of the survey process and was later supported with small group interviews to provide qualitative data.
- Teacher questionnaires which surveyed teachers' attitudes to their schools.
- Parental questionnaires to discover their attitudes towards the school and the relationship between school and parents.

In many cases the research team used or adapted existing questionnaires from other research projects rather than designing new materials. This approach saved time and offered the team the opportunity to refer to other studies.

The case studies were rather different in style. They used ethnographic methods of interviews and observation, which provided added depth to the study and enabled themes to be identified and explored. These included: school ethos, learning and teaching, and leadership. The quantitative and qualitative data gathered were used to triangulate findings and to observe for correlations.

Since the study was concerned with school effectiveness the research team tried to create a dialogue with the schools they were studying so that the leadership teams of the schools could gain something from the process. Each case-study school had two researchers allocated. One researcher had the clear role of conducting research but the other became what the project defined as a 'critical friend', a person who 'asks provocative questions, provides data ... and offers critique...'. The schools varied in their response to this feedback so that some used the data collected to support their efforts to improve whilst others made little use of the research team. While many schools valued the critical friend, there were individual responses to the feedback of data provided by the critical friends that varied from disbelief, to aggression and to defensiveness.

KEY FINDINGS

ATTAINMENT

Differences in pupil attainment seem to be greater among primary schools than secondary schools. The team concluded that early intervention is therefore significant if children are to reach their educational potential. At secondary level, however, pupils' improvement and attainment is significantly related to social background in a way that is less apparent at primary level. There are clear differences between schools at all levels in terms of pupil attainment. The team report that the school is more significant in Scotland in terms of achievement than either social background or factors such as age and gender. Note that this may not be true for the rest of the UK where there is a wider variety of types of schools as a result of Conservative, and later New Labour, educational policies which emphasise choice and variety. More than 96% of Scottish children attend comprehensive schools.

PUPILS

Pupils varied in their concerns and responses according to the schools they attended. They also varied according to their positions in the school as well, so older pupils have a different view of education and their teachers than the younger students within the institution. Pupils reported a sense of a lack of engagement in the decision-making process in many schools, although generally they liked school and believed their teachers aimed to help them.

TEACHERS

Teachers found that the survey process was having an effect on the attitudes and support of their senior-management teams. There were significant differences in perceptions of the school between the senior-management teams and the teachers in a variety of schools. Senior managers had a far more positive view of school than their junior colleagues. The report suggests that many schools need to make a difference to their cultures. Pupils are rewarded in many schools but teachers are not always similarly acknowledged.

PARENTS

Parents generally have a positive view of schools and are more favourable towards primary than secondary schools. There is considerable variation in parental attitudes towards school, with some schools gaining very favourable parent comments and others unfavourable responses. Areas where issues did arise seemed to be ones of communication, work, teacher–pupil relations and the child's response to the school.

OTHER FINDINGS

- There is a general perception that schools in deprived areas are not as good as schools in wealthier areas, even among teachers and often when the statistical evidence shows the opposite result.
- Changing school policy to make a school effective depends on the quality of the management team, the personal enthusiasm of the team leader and the ability of the leader to give the teachers a sense of ownership of the project.
- The role of the 'critical friend' seemed to be helpful to schools, but there were time and geographical problems in the survey as some of the schools were remote. Occasionally the critical friends became the trusted confidantes of the Headteacher and this led to ethical issues that the researchers had to resolve for themselves.

EVALUATION

There are few surprises for anyone involved in education in terms of the conclusions and findings of the study.

Although the book is concerned with educational sociology, it is also a document intended to offer guidance to schools who want to improve. One could guess that very little 'pure' sociology would gain the funding for such a large project because it would not be so closely linked to a topic with such clear relevance for guiding government policy.

Having said that, there are other comments that can be made with reference to the data that is offered.

- There are some tensions in the quantitative data. For instance, bullying is discussed but pupil responses to a self-report question on bullying are recorded with little reference to the controversial nature of defining an act as bullying, or the ability of the bully to recognise his or her own behaviour.
- References to government funding and the implications of lack of funding are made throughout the text. However, the brief of this research is to look at institutions and although the ISEP takes note of the social environment in which the institutions occur, it is not the main theme.
- It is noteworthy that many of the quotations from respondents come from headteachers. While headteachers are significant in implementing change in schools, the judgements of the heads and the junior staff were often different.

QUESTIONS

KNOWLEDGE AND UNDERSTANDING

1. How many schools did the ISEP study in the first stage of the project?
2. How many schools were used in the case-study stage of the project?
3. What were the aims of this research?
4. What was the nature of the 'critical friend' used in the study?
5. Identify two different methods used. Explain why you believe these methods were used.
6. Why did the ISEP tend to rely on developing existing questionnaires and assessment materials for this study?
7. Suggest reasons why large-scale projects such as the ISEP are relatively unusual in Britain.

ANALYSIS

1. What practical problems did the ISEP team face in conducting this study?
2. To what extent can the findings of the ISEP be considered to apply to schools in other cultures and geographical areas, including the rest of the UK?
3. Evaluate the work of the ISEP under each of the following headings: practicality, reliability, ethics, validity, and representativeness.

ISLAM IN TRANSITION:
RELIGION AND IDENTITY AMONG BRITISH PAKISTANI YOUTH

Jessica Jacobson

Routledge, London, 1998

CONTEXT

In this book Jacobson explores the importance of religion in shaping the identities of young British Pakistanis. Although Islam is a minority religion in Britain, it is a dynamic and successful one. This goes against expectation, for it has been widely assumed that in modern societies the institutions (including religion) that were sources of allegiance and authority in traditional societies inevitably decline. Jacobson was interested in Islam as an exception to the general pattern of secularisation. She chose to study British Pakistanis because they are the largest Muslim group in Britain today. She chose to study young people because she wanted to study the second generation, those who had been born and raised in Britain – and thus in an environment in which Islam was a minority religion.

Jacobson's main interest is in identity, and how this is shaped by religion. Her idea of identity is in the symbolic-interactionist tradition started by George Herbert Mead and developed by social psychologists such as Tajfel. Identity here is seen as shaped by interaction between the individual and society, with membership of social groups being an important element of this. Identity is about knowing you belong to a particular group, and the emotional significance of that membership. Identity is, however, not fixed and can vary between situations. The young British Pakistanis Jacobson studied faced what Rex and Josephides called 'identity options', choices between different sources of social identity.

As further background to her study, Jacobson also presents information on British Pakistanis and on the practice of Islam. There are probably between a million and a million and a half Muslims in Britain, about half of whom are Pakistani. Most are Sunni Muslims and follow the Barelvi or Deobandi traditions. About 65% of young Muslims in Britain say they attend a mosque at least once a week, compared with 80% of older respondents. In discussing findings from earlier research about how religion motivates young Pakistanis, Jacobson highlights four themes: the active interest in learning how to be a Muslim; the distinction between ethnicity and religion as sources of identity; the assertion of Muslim identity in protests such as those against the book *The Satanic Verses* by Salman Rushdie; and the development of radical or 'fundamentalist' approaches to Islam. These are followed up in the findings section.

METHODS

The research was carried out over a period of a year in 1992–1993. The research used qualitative methods and took place in the Waltham Forest borough in the East End of London. Working in one area made it possible to relate the answers people gave in interviews to their social environment. Waltham Forest was chosen because of its large Pakistani population. It has the largest Pakistani population of any London borough (13,000, just over 6%, of the borough's population is Pakistani). The Pakistani population of Waltham Forest is also broadly representative of British Pakistanis in terms of age structure and socio-economic status.

The main research method was semi-structured interviews. Respondents were identified using snowball sampling. The interviews were conducted with 33 young British Pakistanis, 18 female and 15 male. All were aged between 17 and 27, and over a half of them were under 20. Three of the boys and three of the girls were married and one of either sex had children. These 'core respondents' included four pairs of siblings, and so they were from 29 different families. Each interview lasted between an hour and two and a half hours. Jacobson used an interview schedule that contained questions covering the main concerns of the research: religion, identity and family and community. All of the interviews were tape-recorded and transcribed, and extracts from them are used throughout the book. Jacobson supplies details of the socio-economic and educational background of her respondents.

Before starting the interviews, she carried out a pilot study with students at the London School of Economics, where she was based while working on her doctoral thesis. The pilot study helped her to identify problems and to find appropriate ways of asking for the information she wanted.

Jacobson also used three additional research methods. First, she interviewed 30 other respondents informally. These were young people from the British Pakistani community in Waltham Forest and from the wider Asian or Muslim population; for example, she made notes of conversations with young men selling Islamic literature at social events. Second, she observed the life of the community through living there during the period of the research. For example, she visited a large number of social events and activities and approached many community organisations. Third, she discussed with 18 local 'community leaders' their views on the concerns of the research and about the younger generation. These supplementary methods enabled her to gain a greater understanding of how the ideas about identity that she heard in the main interviews translated into everyday social life. They also gave her considerable insight into the life of the Pakistani community. The main focus of the book, however, is on young people.

KEY FINDINGS

Ethnicity is a difficult area of identity for young British Pakistanis. They have mixed feelings about seeing themselves as British because they are aware that for many people British means being white and having a British heritage. They feel they are bound to their parents' culture and to other Pakistanis; Pakistani ethnicity seems to be something they cannot escape from.

Yet religious identity is seen differently. Being a Muslim is seen as involving choice and having to be based on reflection, determination and education, and not something you are born into. This emphasis on personal choice is similar to that within Christianity and religious practice in the West in modern times, where it has led to fluid and changeable identities. Jacobson found no evidence for this; rather she found an emphasis on the individual combined with a strong belief in Islam. There is a very strong social boundary between Muslims and non-Muslims, arising from the nature of Islamic thought and the way it provides clear rules for how Muslims should live. Since the Qu'ran is seen as the word of God, the teachings of Islam are seen as unchanging. Thus Islam provides certainties for young people who face much uncertainty in other aspects of their lives, such as their ethnic identity. Jacobson argues that this is the strength of Islam's appeal to young people. Being a Muslim also involves identifying with a global community, unlike an Asian or Pakistani identity.

Jacobson's respondents behaved in ways that reinforced the distinctiveness of their Muslim identities. Even young Muslims who mix socially with non-Muslims tended to keep what Jacobson calls, 'psychological distance'. This construction of boundaries takes many forms, including the following.

- **Formal practices** such as observing Ramadan or attending a mosque
- **Routine behaviour** such as abstaining from alcohol and avoiding non-halal meat

- **General social conduct**: avoiding un-Islamic styles of behaviour such as dating and going to nightclubs
- **Attitudes**: beliefs rather than actions. This showed in the interviews in, for example, disapproval of *The Satanic Verses* by Salman Rushdie even among those who were not strongly committed to Islam.

The importance of these boundaries between Muslim and non-Muslim did not, however, mean that young Muslims retreated into an exclusively Muslim social world (in the way that, for example, the Amish keep themselves separate from mainstream American society). The respondents expected and wanted to work, study and socialise outside as well as inside Muslim circles. The nature of Islam, Jacobson points out, does not encourage exclusivity; Islam is a global and politicised religion that seeks to win converts.

IMPORTANCE This research provides important insights into a complex and potentially controversial area. Many people claim to speak on behalf of minority ethnic groups; here young people from one group are allowed to speak for themselves. The respondents were British born, but facing a wide range of pressures and influences relating to their identities. Jacobson is able to show how ethnic, national and religious identities are related, and to demonstrate that Muslim identities are extremely powerful. Young British Muslims, faced with uncertainties in so many other areas of their lives, find a welcome stability and security in Muslim identities, which they consciously work toward rather simply absorbing them through socialisation within their families. Islam is likely to continue to have a strong appeal for young people from Muslim backgrounds, and thus to be unaffected by the wider secularising trends in British society.

EVALUATION

Jacobson herself identifies two aspects of her research that raise problems. These are representativeness and her status as an outsider.

With regard to representativeness, Jacobson is concerned that her sample may not have been typical of young British Pakistanis in Waltham Forest. She contacted her respondents through snowballing – one respondent suggesting possible others to her – and one consequence of this is that most of her respondents are students contacted through local colleges. There are two other groups she may have missed – those who had broken away from the community and young women from very conservative backgrounds who she was unable to talk to.

Her outsider status raised a number of practical problems. Although she preferred to interview people in their homes, to gain an insight into home life, most respondents lived with their parents, and the older generation were often suspicious of her and of her motives and this could cause difficulties. Where parents did not speak English, Jacobson could not easily reassure them.

'A two-hour interview with another male respondent, Zaheer, was conducted in the front room of his parents' terraced house while his father determinedly swept and swept again the small front yard; in order, or so I assumed, to keep an eye on the proceedings.' (p55)

Jacobson also felt that some respondents were not at ease when talking to her about their experiences of racism because they did not wish to offend her. There was also some suspicion as to why a non-Muslim should be gathering information on Muslims. Jacobson had to find ways of not letting it be assumed that she was thinking of converting to Islam while still encouraging respondents to talk about Islam. On the other hand, she felt that her outsider status was helpful in getting some respondents, especially girls, to talk openly; they felt more relaxed because they did not fear that what they said would be reported to their parents. Others seem to have enjoyed the chance to explain Islam to an outsider.

The relationship between religion and identity for British Pakistanis will change as the social, political, economic and religious context changes. Since Jacobson's research, there have been significant events both within Britain ('riots' in several towns in 2001) and beyond (the terrorist attack on the USA and the subsequent war against the Taliban in Afghanistan). These make it advisable to treat Jacobson's findings as a 'snapshot' of British Pakistanis at the time of the research.

QUESTIONS

KNOWLEDGE AND UNDERSTANDING

1. How many Muslims are there in Britain?
2. Why was Waltham Forest selected for this research?
3. What percentage of Waltham Forest's population are British Pakistanis?
4. What is meant by an 'interview schedule'?
5. In what ways did Jacobson find her pilot study helpful?
6. In what types of ways do young British Pakistanis maintain their Muslim identities?

ANALYSIS

1. How important was it for this research that Jacobson was a white British non-Muslim woman?
2. What problems and issues might arise from the interviews in this research being carried out in the respondents' family homes?
3. Why might the respondents in this research not agree with Jacobson's description of them as 'British Pakistanis'?
4. Evaluate the significance of religion for young British Pakistanis.

References Rex and Josephides (1987) in *Immigrant Associations in Europe* edited by Rex, J, Joly, D and Wilpert, C, Gower, Aldershot

THE EMERGING NETWORK:
A SOCIOLOGY OF THE NEW AGE AND NEO-PAGAN MOVEMENTS

Michael York

Rowman and Littlefield, Lanham, 1995

CONTEXT

This is a study of two linked, and to some extent overlapping, New Religious Movements (NRMs) that have grown over the past twenty years: the New Age Movement and the Neo-pagan movement. The former is sometimes thought of as not having sufficient unity to count as a movement, being instead a multitude of beliefs and practices that can be collectively described as 'New Age'. York accepts that New Age is an umbrella term, covering a wide range of groups and identities, but sees a shared focus on human potential as bringing these together as a movement. The Neo-pagan movement is not easy to distinguish from the New Age movement (see Findings section). York treats them together because of their similarities and because he sees them as constituting a growing phenomenon which acts as an alternative to the Judeo-Christian tradition of the West and to the consumerism, impersonality and environmental degradation of modern society.

Since the two movements studied are new religious movements, part of the sociological context is provided by earlier work on NRMs. Roy Wallis, for example, found that traditional typologies of religious institutions (church, denomination, sect and cult) did not work well for movements founded from the 1960s onwards. He developed a typology of NRMs based on whether they reject, affirm or accommodate themselves to the world. Wallis provides an overview of NRMs in North America, covering, for example, Rajneeshism, EST, Silva Mind Control and the Divine Light Mission. Many NRMs as described by Wallis and others are centred on a strong leader, a 'guru' figure and are authoritarian. The New Age and Neo-pagan movements provided a strong contrast to this, being largely leaderless and anti-authoritarian.

An alternative typology for NRMs is provided by Stark and Bainbridge's distinction between audience cults, client cults and the cult movement (the term 'cult' is being used here to mean a small, new and unconventional grouping; some such groups would in Wallis's typology be sects rather than cults). Stark and Bainbridge's typology is based on the idea of religious compensators and they use it to support their view that NRMs represent a religious revival and are evidence against secularisation. This demonstrates how the debate about how to classify religious organisations is related to wider debates. Other writers have attempted to develop further typologies to distinguish groups within the existing typologies. Bryan Wilson, for example, has suggested seven types of sects, distinguished by their response to the world. Little, however, had been written by sociologists specifically on the New Age and Neo-pagan movements.

METHODS

York used a combination of different methods in the approach known as triangulation. The methods used were participant observation and observation (supported by interviews), questionnaires and the study of secondary data. One general problem he faced was that these movements are different from most other religious organisations. They do not have a hierarchy or recognised spokespeople who could be interviewed. There are no membership lists or (with the exception of initiation into a witches' coven) even a concept of membership. Many people drift in and out, attending occasional talks or workshops, and it would be difficult to claim they were all 'New Agers'. Nor do the movements have clear sets of beliefs or practices.

The participant observation took place in various settings. York attended, for example, gatherings at The House of the Goddess where pagans, witches and occultists met, and went to a series of evening lectures, St James' Alternatives. Because he was trying to obtain as complete as possible a picture of the movement, he tried to observe as many different venues, workshops, assemblies and so on as possible. He found that gaining access to meetings and events was not a problem, though finding out where to go (and when) could be, especially in the early stages, since information was often passed around by word of mouth.

York found that his participant observation followed the three stages outlined by Eileen Barker in her study of the Unification Church (also known as the Moonies). The first stage of his participation and observation was passive, the second interactive, the third active. He progressed from concentrating on observing, getting a feel for the social situation, then gradually grew in knowledge and confidence so that he was able first to play a small part, asking occasional questions, and then to fully participate.

Neo-pagan meetings were more difficult than New Age meetings. New Age meetings were usually very open, while Neo-pagan meetings involved more ceremony and rituals. Tape-recording and notes were not allowed during rituals, because all present were supposed to be fully involved; participants were welcome, but not observers. Afterwards, however, Neo-pagans would help York write notes on what had happened.

York distributed questionnaires to try to develop a profile on both New Agers and Neo-pagans. He collected information from people attending meetings about their occupation, income, family life, background, religion, sexual orientation and self-perception. He asked about three issues that were contentious at the time: nuclear energy, abortion and AIDS, to try to see whether New Agers and Neo-pagans had a distinctive stance. Finally, he asked about how much respondents knew about New Religious Movements, how they would classify them, how much they knew about the New Age or Neo-pagan movements and how involvement had affected their lives. He combined his findings with those of earlier research

KEY FINDINGS

New Agers and Neo-pagans (obtained from questionnaire research) tended to be drawn from mainstream middle-class occupations (particularly teaching), arts and crafts, writing and related work. There was, however, considerable variation between the different samples, reflecting in part the small numbers involved. Most respondents had had some education beyond compulsory schooling. Most had also been brought up in Protestant families, although the St James' Alternatives respondents contained a higher proportion of former Jews than might have been expected. When respondents were asked about their religion there was a wide variety of responses. Among the St James' Alternatives respondents, 23% said they had no religious identity and only 8% described themselves as New Age, other responses included 'Buddhist', 'neo-Christian Buddhist', 'Hindu', 'my own path' and 'any and all pathways'. A question about belief in God showed that respondents did almost all believe in some kind of God or force, but with a very wide range of conceptions of God.

In looking at how individuals had been affected by participation in the movements, York uses selective quotations. Reasons given for involvement included, 'becoming more aware of internal processes within oneself', 'interesting people and activities' and 'loss of feelings of isolation'. An idea that recurred in responses was the idea that God could be found both inside and outside you.

The differences cited between the New Age and Neo-pagan movements are that the New Age movement sees itself as new and distinct whereas the Neo-pagan movement sees itself as based on an ancient but often suppressed tradition, stressing its continuity with the past. 'Whereas New Age is self-styled as an awakening, Neo-paganism thinks of itself more as a re-awakening' (p2). Neo-pagan ceremonies involve greater use of rituals, which are intended to produce an altered state of consciousness.

York provides accounts of some of his participant observation at different venues and meetings. Here is an extract from his account of the Pagan Moon ceremony on 10 March 1990 to give a flavour of these:

> 'Shan (the Clan Mother) now bade us walk briskly in a circular counter-clockwise fashion. Eventually, during a second stage, the pace was slowed to a slow walk. A third stage consisted of the slowest movement possible... One large circle was re-formed. Shan had selected four men to invoke the elements. I was asked and chose to call forth fire, the ruler of the south... Shan had explained that it did not matter what we said... but she asked that since I had selected fire I make the invocation correspondingly dramatic and powerful. I identified fire as the power of vitality, warmth and light and bid this 'guardian' to come to our circle – bringing therewith enlightenment... During my invocation to the element of fire, the group collectively snapped their fingers.' (p226)

One of York's aims was to investigate to what extent the church–sect typology and later adaptations of it fitted the New Age and Neo-pagan movements. This aim was based on recognition that the two movements were in several important ways different from other NRMs that had been studied. With some qualifications, he concludes that as a whole the New Age is best described by Stark and Bainbridge's concept of the 'audience cult', the most diffuse and least organised kind of cult. To categorise Neo-paganism, he turns to Bryan Wilson's lesser-known typology of sects, seeing it as combining the characteristics of thaumaturgical and manipulationist sects. Wilson describes thaumaturgical sects as involving religion and magic and typical of pre-literate societies although they can arise in more advanced societies. Manipulationist sects are focused on achievement in the world, building confidence and well-being among members and offering an alternative to the pressure to compete for power and success. Neither movement, however, clearly fits into a neat slot in any typology. This shows that the typologies need to be treated not as providing fixed compartments into which religious movements must be made to fit, but as working tools to be used or discarded according to how useful they are in attempts to capture and describe the reality.

IMPORTANCE This book provides a wealth of ideas and information describing the New Age and Neo-pagan movements, which are not yet well documented in sociological texts. It provides a useful illustration of the range of methods that can be used in research religious movements, and of the usefulness or otherwise of the various typologies of religious movements. Its use of findings from other earlier research helps build a clearer picture of the movements.

EVALUATION

Perhaps inevitably, York uses a large number of abbreviations and it is easy to become confused as one tries to follow which movement or set of ideas he is writing about; he could also be clearer when explaining, for example, the various typologies. The conclusion chapter brings in new ideas and writers, rather than providing a summary of York's own findings. The descriptions of the movements and their followers tend to be overshadowed by thorough but inconclusive descriptions of a large number of sources.

With regard to methodology, research of this kind raises problems in the areas of representativeness and validity that are difficult to overcome. In the case of the questionnaires, the samples were inevitably very small, and the findings not necessarily representative of any wider group. The nature of these movements is that they do not have a hierarchical organisation or membership lists. The researcher has to decide what beliefs, practices or events and meetings count as 'New Age' or 'Neo-pagan'. While York is arguing for the existence of a New Age movement, his findings arguably show that groups within this movement are very different from one other – for example, in their social composition. The participant-observation accounts are fascinating but brief and, by their nature, not necessarily typical of other New Age or Neo-pagan gatherings. The presence of York, known to be a researcher, may also have affected the behaviour of those present.

QUESTIONS

KNOWLEDGE AND UNDERSTANDING

1. What is the term given to the use of a combination of different methods?
2. What is meant by the term 'New Age'?
3. What are the four categories (types) in Wallis' original typology of religious organisations?
4. Why did Wallis later modify this typology?
5. What three stages did both York and, earlier, Barker, find that their participant observation was divided into?
6. Identify five New Religious Movements.

ANALYSIS

1. Why might particular groups of people be attracted to the New Age and Neo-pagan movements?
2. To what extent can the New Age be described as a single, coherent movement?
3. Evaluate the usefulness of the different types of data on New Religious Movements that might be generated by (a) a survey questionnaire and (b) participant observation.
4. Discuss the usefulness of different typologies of religious organisations.

References
Barker, E (1984), *The Making of a Moonie*, Blackwell, Oxford
Stark, W S and Bainbridge, W A (1985), *The Future of Religion*, University of California Press, Berkeley
Wallis, R (1984), *The Elementary Forms of the New Religious Life*, Routledge, London
Wilson, B (1970), *Religious Sects*, Weidenfeld and Nicholson, London

'NEITHER HERE NOR THERE':
THE CONSTRUCTION OF IDENTITIES AND BOUNDARY MAINTENANCE OF WEST AFRICAN PENTECOSTALS

Stephen Hunt

Sociology, Volume 36 Number 1, (February 2002)

CONTEXT

The argument for secularisation contends that there has been a decline in the significance of religion in people's lives in the industrialised world today. While this seems to be true to some extent for Britain, we need to look at how some forms of religion have grown and are of central importance to their followers. While the traditional Christian denominations have declined, other world religions (such as Islam and Buddhism) have grown in Britain, as have some new religious movements. Hunt's research looks at one particular non-traditional Christian movement, Pentecostalism, and in particular at a new variety of Pentecostalism popular among people in Britain of Nigerian origin.

Pentecostalism has previously been studied by sociologists such as Cashmore and Pryce whose main concern was ethnicity rather than religion. They were interested in how membership of a religious group could be a means for first-generation immigrants to adapt and find support. Pryce, in his participant-observation study of West Indian communities in the St Paul's area of Bristol, attended Pentecostal services – which he found exhausting. Pentecostal services are very different from the practices of traditional Christian denominations in that they involve considerable audience participation, call and response and members 'speaking in tongues' under the influence, they believe, of the Holy Spirit.

Black Pentecostalism and similar religious movements among immigrant communities have normally been explained as adaptations to experiences in Western society. Cashmore and Pryce described the growth of Pentecostalism among first-generation West Indians in Britain as filling a need for community and moral guidance in alien surroundings. Faced with discrimination, even hostility, in work and other areas of life, and feeling unwelcome in British churches, one response of black people was to turn to forms of Christianity that provided a strong sense of community and belonging. Pentecostalism was a form of religious compensation for alienated groups.

Hunt adopts a somewhat different focus; he is more concerned with the ways in which Pentecostalism helps people to construct identities. A recent development in sociology is to see identities as being constructed. Class, gender, age, nationality, religion and other factors are seen as resources people can draw on in constructing identities, rather than as aspects of social structure imposed on people. Identities constantly shift, they are not fixed. This ties in with the idea of a 'spiritual marketplace', associated with postmodernism. People, it is argued, are able to select their religious beliefs and practices from the wide range now available. They will select those that best suit their lifestyle and experience. This is often expressed in terms of people finding their own truths, their own spirituality, and so on. Hunt is interested in why Pentecostalism appeals to Nigerians in Britain and how they use it to help construct their religious, national, ethnic identities – and perhaps other identities too, such as class and gender.

METHODS

Hunt's research looks at a later wave of Pentecostalism than that studied by earlier writers, and at churches with largely Nigerian rather than Caribbean congregations.

Hunt's research involved 50 semi-structured interviews with members of the Redeemed Christian Church of God (RCCG). This West African version of Pentecostalism is, according to Hunt, one of the fastest-growing religious movements in Britain, with a membership of about 170,000 in London and other large towns and cities. It claims membership of more than a million around the world. The church originated and remains based in Nigeria, and its significant presence in Britain reflects the historical colonial connection between the two countries. Hunt discovered that the RCCG was different in significant ways from older Pentecostal churches both in Nigeria and in Britain.

Hunt's interviews were carried out with members of the church's largest congregation in Britain, which is based at the Jesus House (a former BBC warehouse) and has about 1,500 adult members. The semi-structured interviews were conducted at the Jesus House, each lasting about one hour. Half were face-to-face interviews, half focus-group interviews. The interviews were designed to build upon information already gathered by questionnaire, which covered social background, personal life, work, church activities and religious orientation. The interviews were concerned with exploring how church members constructed religious identities in relation to both past and current experiences and aspirations for the future.

Hunt also carried out a content analysis of church publications. There was a wide range of these available, because of the church's mission to evangelise – that is, to recruit new members. The church has, however, not been successful in recruiting people other than of Nigerian origin.

KEY FINDINGS

Hunt argues that the conventional interpretation of Pentecostalism as a response to experiences of discrimination and marginalisation in the West misses out the importance of experiences in countries of origin, in this case Nigeria. The distinct identities that people create bring together past experiences in Nigeria with their current situation in Britain.

Ways in which the church had changed in Nigeria made it successful in Britain. The RCCG's mother church in Nigeria had undergone transformations during a turbulent period in Nigerian history in the 1980s and 1990s when a collapse in oil prices led to sharp falls in living standards and was followed by the imposition of Structural Adjustment Programmes. The church grew rapidly in Nigeria because it was able to offer resources and support and to give people a belief in self-improvement. Thus the church developed to provide its members with ways of coping with Nigerian life but, in so doing, also made itself helpful to Nigerians in Britain trying to adapt to a different set of conditions.

While church members are integrated at work and at college with other ethnic groups, the church provided a setting for gathering with people from the same nation and culture.

MEMBERSHIP

96% of respondents described themselves as African and 90% as Nigerian. Many were from privileged backgrounds in Nigeria. Whereas older Pentecostal churches in Nigeria have a large following among the poor, the newer churches such as the RCCG also attract more affluent and upwardly mobile urban groups. The Nigerian population in Britain is largely drawn from this group and this is reflected in the RCCG sample, which was young (93% under 41) and middle class (65% in professional occupations). 65% had degrees and/or professional qualifications. About a third of the sample was not in employment and 80% of these were students. The congregation was then composed mainly of young people, fairly affluent and developing their careers in Britain. This contrasts both with mainstream British religion and with the older Pentecostal churches which have mainly middle-aged and elderly congregations.

The majority of the sample was single, and less than a third had children, which together indicate a large number not having a settled family life in Britain. Many were 'sojourners', spending time away from Nigeria studying and working, but expecting to return to Nigeria. This partly reflects the status of Nigerian higher education; Nigerian middle-class parents prefer to send their children to the West to study because they believe the Nigerian education system has declined.

ETHNICITY AND NATIONALITY

The great majority of the respondents had been practising Christians in a variety of churches in Nigeria. In Britain they gave up those allegiances and turned to the RCGG through finding out about it through relatives or friends. The RCGG allowed young Nigerians in particular to develop an identity as an age cohort as well as in terms of ethnicity and nationality. Young members felt they were allowed greater personal freedom in the RCGG than in churches in Nigeria. They were rather ambivalent towards Nigeria; they saw much wrong with life there and with traditional ways of life, but it remained home for most, and a place they intended to return to.

GENDER

The RCGG had an even higher percentage of female members (71%) than in most British churches, and this affected church organisation and socialising within the church. Although there was deference to male leadership, women were in positions to influence and take decisions and there was a more egalitarian ethos. There were also informal women-only groups within the church based on particular interests, such as the female youth group ('Rock Squad'), the 'Singles' (looking for a partner) and the 'Good Women Fellowship' (for married women). The church provided a setting for Nigerian women in Britain to create a close network of support, encouraging hard work, creativity and career advancement. The women interviewed had egalitarian outlooks and moderately feminist views, although these were modified in their ideas of a future based on marriage and the family, and of what God might want them to do. Hunt's content analysis of church literature found quite a strong emphasis on women finding the right partner.

Church teachings fitted in with the aspirations of the young, professional congregation. Hunt refers to these as 'prosperity teachings', which promote hard work, materialism and success through effort. Church literature offers advice on achievement in this world, stressing that God wanted people to be successful in all areas of life, not just to improve themselves spiritually. Seminars and practical advice on money and debt were available. RCCG members wanted to distance themselves from the image of Nigerian society as corrupt.

While these prosperity teachings fitted well with the material aspirations of much of mainstream society, religion also played a role in creating boundaries between the church members and the world outside. The RCCG emphasised the 'differentness' of its congregation. One aspect of this was a stress on purity and cleanliness, again as a distancing from the image of Nigeria but also as a distancing from British society, which was seen as marked by family breakdown, a lack of respect for others and promiscuity.

One of the reasons for the success of the new Pentecostalism, Hunt suggests, is that it has moved away from the sectarian and millenarian nature of Caribbean Pentecostalism towards an emphasis on values such as success, having a career and realising one's potential. These are also Western values, and they enable followers to avoid resignation and despair through encouraging the search for ways to improve life. A version of the Protestant work ethic described by Weber survives here.

IMPORTANCE

Hunt draws attention to some aspects of religion in an age of globalisation. The spread of Pentecostalism in Britain is in itself an interesting illustration of global cultural exchanges: Christianity exported to Nigeria, blended with aspects of Nigerian culture and then seeking to evangelise in the West (though so far with little success among the white population). While the overall trend in Britain may be towards secularisation, Hunt's findings give an account of a growth area, with a particular form of religion thriving because it suits the needs and aspirations of a particular group. While traditional religiosity continues to decline, religious movements outside the mainstream find space to grow. At the very least, this provides a cautionary note against the predictions of continuing religious decline.

Hunt's work extends the sociology of religion into new areas suggested by postmodern thinking. The idea of a spiritual marketplace in which people can 'pick and mix' religion has gained currency, but Hunt goes beyond this to ask why particular types of people choose particular forms of religion, and what uses they then make of religion in constructing their identities.

EVALUATION Hunt's is a case study of one particular congregation of one church, and therefore we need to be cautious about making any assumptions about the extent to which the findings apply to other churches or to Pentecostalism more generally. The church members were also ethnically distinct, and we should not make assumptions about the relationship between religion and identities for other minority ethnic groups.

Hunt's main concern is the ways in which the church members used their religion to help them construct identities. This leads naturally to an emphasis on the ability of people to construct their own identities. What this leaves out is the ways in which choices are constrained; there is scope for agency, but within boundaries determined by wider social structures. In this case the boundaries would include the institutional racism of churches. It is not only Pentecostal churches that have congregations made up overwhelmingly of one ethnic group, but the mainstream churches as well.

QUESTIONS

KNOWLEDGE AND UNDERSTANDING

1 What is the conventional explanation for the popularity of Pentecostalism among African-Caribbeans?
2 What is meant by a 'focus group'?
3 What is meant by a 'sojourner'?
4 How did religious beliefs affect the feminism of female RCCG members?
5 What does Hunt mean by 'prosperity teachings' and why might these appeal to Nigerians in Britain?
6 What aspects of Nigerian life did RCGG members tend to reject or disapprove of?

ANALYSIS

1 Why was the membership of the RCGG different (in terms of class, age and gender) from the membership of other churches in Britain?
2 In what ways does the Pentecostalism of the RCGG differ from the earlier Pentecostalism of the first generation of West Indian settlers in Britain?
3 Assess the usefulness of focus-group interviews in researching church congregations.
4 Is religion likely to continue to play an important role in helping construct ethnic identities in Britain? Give reasons for your answer.

References Cashmore, E (1989), *United Kingdom?* Unwin Hyman, London

Pryce, K (1979), *Endless Pressure*, Penguin, Harmondsworth

THE KENDAL PROJECT:
PATTERNS OF THE SACRED IN CONTEMPORARY SOCIETY

Research carried out by members of the Department of Religious Studies at Lancaster University

Unpublished work in progress. Web site: http://ktru-main.lancs.ac.uk/ieppp/kendal.nsf

CONTEXT

This project was designed to address four ongoing debates in the study of religion and spirituality in Britain: secularisation; believing and belonging; the sacralisation of alternative spirituality theory; and the spiritual revolution thesis. These, to differing extents, contradict each other and so cannot all be true. They will be considered one by one.

- **Secularisation** refers to the idea that while society used to be religious, organised religion is now in decline and the majority of people do not believe or do not practise a religion any more. Secularisation was predicted, for different reasons, by both Durkheim and Marx. One of the reasons why secularisation remains a controversial idea is that there is no agreement on how to measure it. Measurements of most aspects of religious belief and practice do indicate a decline in religion in most of Western Europe during the twentieth century, but this is not a global pattern, and religion remains a significant force within the United Kingdom in Northern Ireland.
- **Believing and belonging**. An argument related to secularisation has been put forward by Grace Davie, who has argued that people today may still believe in religion while not belonging to formal religious organisations. Davie cites as evidence of the continuing importance of religious feelings such recent events as the public responses to the death of Princess Diana and to the Hillsborough stadium disaster. Davie acknowledges that religious practice – as measured, for example, by church membership and attendance figures – is in long-term decline but says that British people continue to agree with general statements of belief in some kind of supernatural being and to turn to religion in times of stress. So, by what can be called 'soft' religious variables (statements of belief or of being spiritually inclined) religion remains significant while by 'harder' variables (such as regular church attendance) it is in decline. People continue to believe but no longer in large numbers belong to religious organisations.
- **The sacralisation or alternative spirituality thesis**. This is the argument that although Christianity is a spent force, alternative forms of spirituality such as New Age beliefs are becoming more widespread and more important. Very large numbers now have some interest or belief in some New Age ideas. This can be seen as related to the decline of the Western worldview established during the Enlightenment and to the growth of a more postmodern outlook with a multiplicity of beliefs and practices from which people can select, dipping in and out without permanent commitment.
- **The spiritual revolution thesis**. This argument accepts the decline of organised religion but sees it as being replaced not by secularity but by a more spiritual outlook. This is seen as happening within established religions as well as within

New Age and alternative spirituality. Thus, the nature of religion has changed – from belief in a set of forces shaping our lives to the idea of the sacred being present in the world and in people's ability to realise their own spirituality and transform their lives. This argument is also sometimes referred to as the 'turn to life', because religion has become focused on this world, on personal consciousness and the here and now rather than on heaven, the afterlife and so on.

METHODS

The Kendal Project is based on the idea that since all four of these arguments are being put forward, and cannot all be true, the empirical evidence from large-scale studies is not helping resolve the issues. The decision was made to go deeper by testing the ideas in one place, by a locality study. The town of Kendal was chosen for both academic and practical reasons. It is close to Lancaster, where the researchers are based, and it is the right size to have a wide range of religious activities yet to be fully covered by the project. Kendal has a church-attendance rate slightly above the national average and is also a centre for New Age and alternative spirituality beliefs. It therefore offered opportunities to explore the issues the researchers were interested in.

The research had two main areas of focus: a church and chapel study and a study of alternative spiritualities. The church and chapel study involved:

- a count of everyone attending churches and chapels on a particular Sunday
- a questionnaire survey at all religious institutions
- in-depth studies of three Christian communities using ethnographic fieldwork (attending services and events), interviews with individuals and focus-group discussions.

The study of alternative spiritualities involved:
- identifying new spiritual outlets and assessing the extent of their use
- interviews with therapists and spiritual teachers to get a better idea of who uses their services
- in-depth studies of three spiritual outlets – again, using ethnographic fieldwork, interviews with practitioners and clients and focus-group discussions.

Supplementary research included a study of religious literature sold in Kendal (for example, what was stocked in bookshops) and a street survey. The street survey involved a doorstep survey of 100 households in a part of Kendal with a wide range of housing, follow-up semi-structured interviews with 30 households and in-depth ethnographic visits to ten households.

For the church and chapel research, the first task was to obtain a list of all churches. The next stage was to attend a service at each and observe and describe it. The researcher followed a checklist, arriving at the venue half an hour or so before a service, introducing herself to the 'greeter' on the door and asking permission to observe the service and take notes. As well as describing the physical setting, notes were made about what happened when people arrived and what the leaders and the congregation did. She also collected any literature available. Attending a service at each church was very time consuming; there were 26 churches and this meant 26 fieldwork days over 26 weeks because in almost all cases the visit could only be on a Sunday. It was also important that the service attended was typical, and that the field notes were sufficient to enable appropriate churches to be identified for the later case studies.

For the attendance count, a form was used divided into male and female and by age. Counting was done as people arrived, because inside churches accurate counts were difficult when some people were hidden by furniture. To carry out counts at all churches on the same day the research team recruited undergraduate students who were paid a small fee. A student was placed at each entrance and told to stay in place until ten minutes after the service had started so as to include latecomers. Counts were also taken at afternoon and evening services, and the researchers tried to find out from clergy how many of these were 'double attenders', who had also attended a morning service, so as not to include them twice in a final count of total numbers attending churches on that day.

The ethnographic case studies were not fully ethnographic in the sense that the researcher did not fully participate and observe. The researcher attended some services and events and carried out long semi-structured interviews in which respondents were encouraged to speak freely. She also spoke to other people informally. The observations and questions were focused on such issues as what church members got from being members, their beliefs and the relationship between the church and their lives. In each of the four cases the researcher gained permission from 'gate-keepers' to carry out the research and in three cases made a presentation during a service to explain her presence.

KEY FINDINGS

This project is not yet complete and the findings given here should not be taken as final.

CHURCH AND CHAPEL

There were 25 congregations. The researchers defined congregation as a group regarding itself as a distinct community so, for example, two groups of Jehovah's Witnesses meeting in the same place at different times on Sundays were counted as two congregations.

The researchers developed a typology of churches and chapels' degrees of humanisation (turning to the human rather than the divine) and subjectivisation (turning to a focus on own life). They distinguished the following.

- **Hard**: low humanisation, low subjectivisation; e.g. Jehovah's Witnesses, evangelical churches.
- **Medium-hard**: low humanisation, high subjectivisation; e.g. Salvation Army, Christian Science, some Church of England churches.
- **Medium-soft**: high humanisation, low subjectivisation; e.g. Methodist, United Reform, Roman Catholic, other Church of England.
- **Soft**: high humanisation, high subjectivisation; e.g. Unitarian, Spiritualist church, Quakers.

These types of churches have different appeals to people. The hard and medium-hard churches offer strong communities with a strong sense of belonging to a group, appealing to those who do not feel at home in modern society and are in search of a home. The medium-soft churches appeal to those who do feel at home in contemporary society, while soft churches are about continuing to feel homeless, following your own spiritual journey but offering some sense of community.

Total church attendance on 26 November 2000, the day of the attendance count, was 2,207, out of a total population of 27,610, which is 8%. More than half of all church attenders attended a medium-soft church. The female to male ratio was 1.5 to 1; this varied between churches but not significantly between types of churches. Under-eighteens made up 16.8% of the attenders, but only 2.8% of attenders at soft churches, which raises questions about socialisation of the next generation.

Oral history evidence suggested a fall in numbers but some churches had increased recently. These were at both ends of the hard/soft spectrum – evangelical churches and Jehovah's Witnesses (who had had to divide into two congregations to accommodate growing numbers) at the hard end, but also Unitarians and Quakers at the soft end. Although their numbers remained high as total proportions, it was the more mainstream 'liberal' congregations in the middle of the spectrum that were in decline.

ALTERNATIVE SPIRITUALITIES

There were 62 spiritual groups meeting regularly in and within five miles of Kendal. 24 of these met in centres offering alternative spiritualities, 19 in more general public centres, nine in other rented venues and ten in people's homes. They included 23 yoga groups, seven Tai Chi groups and many other smaller and more specialised groups. There were also 63 one-to-one practitioners. There were seven spiritual centres, two of which were accessible to the public. About 750 people in all were involved, between 2% and 3% of the population; 80% of these were women. 26 groups had been running for less than five years, but it was not possible to find out how long 15 of the groups had been running.

There were 63 one-to-one practitioners known publicly or at least within complementary therapy social networks; the figures exclude those who practise only privately with family and friends because it would be almost impossible to find out about this. 39% had been practising for less than five years.

Most of those involved were over forty, with only one one-to-one practitioner being under 30. It seems to be not the 1960s generation themselves but the immediate post-1960s generation who are most attracted to alternative spiritualities. They were perhaps influenced by older siblings and friends to be more open to these ideas. This age profile may be very significant, for it suggests the possibility that New Age spiritual alternatives may turn out to be significant only for one, now ageing, age cohort, and may die out.

There had been a very definite increase in numbers, starting from very little activity at all in 1970. This is confirmed by asking people and by, for example, counting Yellow Pages listings.

IMPORTANCE The project, while unfinished, has already shed light on an area of intense debate. By focusing on just one locality (which may well, of course, not be representative) the researchers are able to gauge the strength both of religion as practised in churches and chapels and of alternative spiritualities. The evidence is used to assess four theories of the significance of belief today, with tentative results that point to areas for further research.

EVALUATION

Since the main purpose of the research was to assess the validity of the four arguments listed in the context section above, clearly the findings must be related to these. Again, it must be remembered that the findings presented are only from initial stages of the research, which at the time of writing remains unfinished.

The findings on church and chapel attendance generally support the claim that religion as measured by church attendance is in decline, but there were areas of growth or of stability. The findings do not give support to the 'believing but not belonging' or 'alternative spirituality' theses. With regard to the 'turn to life' thesis, congregations that draw on spirituality (for example, in emphasising the Holy Spirit) are doing well, yet equally so are those that concentrate on the life to come.

Alternative spiritualities do seem to be growing, but at only 2–3% of the population involved this growth would not discredit the secularisation argument. There is some support for the sacralisation of alternative spirituality thesis; however, the project has not yet looked at how many people who are not involved in one-to-one alternative practices are drawing on alternative resources – for example, by reading mind, body and spirit books.

The evidence for changes over time is less than certain, being based mainly on interviews and therefore on people's memories. This is supported by counting, for example, advertisements, yet there is a problem here in that alternative practices may have been widespread and publicised informally before some practitioners took the step of advertising to a wider public.

Bringing the two areas together, there are about 10–11% of the population involved in either church/chapel or alternative spiritualities. Given the decline of most of the church/chapel congregations, this is almost certainly a lower figure than in the recent past. It also leaves almost 90% of the population not involved. The street survey should provide some information on people who were not reached by the initial church and alternative-spiritualities research.

QUESTIONS

KNOWLEDGE AND UNDERSTANDING

1. Why was the town of Kendal chosen for this project?
2. Which sociologist is associated with the 'believing but not belonging' argument?
3. How many congregations were there in Kendal? Why is it not as straightforward to count them as you might think?
4. Draw a diagram to illustrate the typology of churches used in this project. Include examples.
5. What was the ratio of male to female church attenders?
6. Approximately what percentage of Kendal's population are involved in alternative spiritualities?
7. Approximately what percentage of Kendal's population are not involved in religious or spiritual practices?

ANALYSIS

1. Evaluate the likelihood of alternative spiritualities continuing to grow in terms of numbers involved.
2. Evaluate the reasons why some church congregations are growing or stable while others are declining.
3. Discuss the problems involved in carrying out a count of church attendance in one town on one day.

References Davie, G (1994), *Religion in Britain since 1945: Believing without Belonging*, Blackwell, Oxford

TV LIVING

David Gauntlett and Annette Hill

Routledge, London, 1999

CONTEXT

This book presents the findings of a British Film Institute project – the Audience Tracking Study – that involved the questioning of 500 respondents over a five-year period. Questions concerned their lives, their television viewing and the relationship between the two.

The first major qualitative study of people's television viewing in their homes was by David Morley in his book *Family Television* (1986). Earlier, Morley had studied how audiences responded to a particular programme, *Nationwide*, and argued that people's responses were determined by their socio-economic position – basically, their class. Morley later realised that showing groups of people a programme they might not have watched could itself create responses. He became interested in finding out how people actually watched in the context of their own homes. The family or household context was important because people do not watch TV as isolated individuals. His research for *Family Television* only involved 18 households – a small and unrepresentative sample – yet the book has become very influential, particularly for its discovery of striking differences between men and women in television viewing. Morley found, for example, that men like to watch television uninterrupted and in silence, while women typically combine television viewing with other activities including conversation.

A qualitative study that provides a more direct precedent for the Audience Tracking Study is *Watching Dallas* by Ien Ang (1985). Ang also asked her respondents (fans of the 1970s American soap saga *Dallas*) to write about their viewing of television. This was one of the first studies to treat seriously and sympathetically audiences for popular media, and to allow audiences to express themselves in their own words and at length.

These ethnographic studies of audiences reflected a shift in thinking about media effects but all were limited in size and scope. The Audience Tracking Study was the largest project of its type in sample size, the amount of information collected and the duration of the study.

The research took place after the 1990 Broadcasting Act, which had prepared the way for multi-channel television. It therefore took place at an important time in the development of British television, and the findings should be seen in the context of that time. In 1991 59% of respondents had at least one video recorder in their household, by 1996 this had risen to 87%. The percentage with satellite or cable, and therefore multi-channel, television rose from seven to 26. A set of ideas about these changes that was gaining support at the time of the research was the theory of the 'fragmented audience'. It was thought that viewing would cease to be a shared activity, with each family or household member watching their own choice of programme on niche channels on their own television, away from other people.

METHODS

This research had its origins in the 1988 *One Day in the Life of Television* project. This involved 22,000 people, recruited through advertisements (a self-selected sample), writing a diary about their television viewing on 1 November 1988. The British Film Institute followed this up, choosing a sample of just over 500 people from the original sample who were generally representative of the British population, taking into account sex, age, marital status, region, occupation and household size and composition.

The survey was longitudinal and ran from 1991 to 1996, with respondents completing 15 questionnaire diaries, three a year. 427 out of 509 respondents were involved throughout the five years – quite a good success rate. One way the researchers maintained contact between each request for diary entries was to send birthday and Christmas cards, and also to write personally when diaries disclosed developments such as bereavement or serious illness.

Respondents were asked structured questions relating to television viewing, the nature of the household and daily routines, and also questions about particular programmes or topical issues. The questionnaire also included open-ended questions. The style of questioning was designed to encourage respondents to reflect upon their viewing in the context of their lives. Respondents kept a viewing chart on which they noted what they had watched, with whom, how much attention they had given to the programme and whether they had planned to watch it. Diaries were requested in different months in different years to ensure coverage of seasonal variations, and were set for different days of the week. Over the period of the research the respondents submitted a total of three and a half million words. In analysing the data Gauntlett and Hill tried to be led by the respondents' interests and priorities rather than their own.

KEY FINDINGS

The nature of research of this type is that it illuminates many different aspects of the topic studied rather than leading to a single major conclusion. Each of eight chapters in the book presents a series of key findings, often running to ten points or more. A brief summary is given here.

- **Television and everyday life**
  Television programmes provide fixed points that help people structure their daily lives. Many people watch programmes at weekends that they would not watch during the week when there is more pressure on their time. Television viewing can help bond a family or household (such as a group of students) but can also be a source of disputes and irritation.
- **News consumption and everyday life**
  Watching the news is often part of a daily routine, and within families young adults develop an interest in the news from the example of parents. Both men and women are interested in the news but women are less likely to be able to find time to watch.
- **Transitions and change**
  Adults have more established viewing patterns than young adults. Television can be used to reduce stress in times of crisis; television viewing then tends to be reduced after the crisis. Transitions in life (such as leaving home and going to university) disrupt viewing habits.
- **Television's personal meanings**
  Television means different things to different people. For some it is a valuable 'window on the world', for others 'electronic wallpaper'. Television can be a valuable source of companionship, and many people also value being able to talk about viewing afterwards.
- **Video and technology in the home**
  Video machines were used regularly by people of all ages and were used in many

ways, such as collecting material for children and for viewing without having to watch advertisements. There was little evidence of the division in video use by gender that Morley reported.

- **The retired and elderly audiences**
  The retired and elderly are not a homogenous group; they have very varied tastes and viewing habits. They share the experience of having grown up without television. Many value television as a way of keeping them informed and mentally active. Older people tend to prefer more 'gentle' and 'pleasant' programmes than younger viewers, especially those that support a view of the world as they would like to remember it.

- **Gender and television**
  Many respondents rejected the idea that men and women had different viewing interests. Younger women and many men found daytime television insulting. Soap operas were not a 'female genre', as some academics have claimed; many men watched them and were fully engaged by them. A minority of respondents objected to gay and lesbian lifestyles being shown and this was usually combined with other prejudices such as racism. Men did use the remote-control more than women (as Morley had found) but only after consulting with other family members.

- **Television violence and other controversies**
  There was more concern about fictional violence than about other potentially controversial television. Respondents felt children needed to be protected from violence, sex, nudity and bad language and approved of the nine o'clock watershed. Some criticised news reporting of tragedies such as the Dunblane shootings for lack of sensitivity.

The researchers felt that although the 1990 Broadcasting Act was seen as tremendously important by politicians and broadcasters, it had had little effect on viewing – even by the end of the research period. For example, TV-AM lost its franchise for broadcasting breakfast television on ITV in 1993; but the researchers comment, '…this was quite earth-shattering in the broadcasting industry, and even in Westminster… But as far as the consumer is concerned, TV-AM and GMTV are like two makes of cola, bubbly but basically indistinguishable, and probably bad for you.' (page 285)

Gauntlett and Hill reject the idea of the 'fragmented audience'. Even in the small minority of households with cable or satellite television, viewing remained a family activity.

IMPORTANCE The scale of the research and the sample selection, despite its imperfections, makes this the most important ethnographic study of television audiences. By quoting extensively from the diaries, Gauntlett and Hill gain real insights into television viewing in families. The results are sometimes surprising and dispel misleading ideas derived from earlier and much smaller-scale research, such as the strong gender divide that Morley had found. Despite the timing of the research just after the Broadcasting Act, the research found more continuity than change from the pre-1990 period of restricted public-service television. Although multi-channel television has grown rapidly since 1996, this research suggests that we should be cautious about claims that the nature of television viewing has been transformed and fragmented.

EVALUATION

A major problem with this research is its sheer scale. It generated a phenomenal amount of data, and while the researchers wanted to let viewers speak for themselves they inevitably had to sort and prioritise responses, for example, in choosing those to quote from in this book. This was an inevitable outcome of producing so much data.

The sampling frame used – participants in *One Day in the Life of Television* – was self-selected and cannot be taken to be representative of the British population. Young people and (probably) minority ethnic groups were under-represented, and the middle classes over-represented. Although the sample for the Audience Tracking Study was chosen for characteristics that made it representative, the individuals had all volunteered for the initial research. The quotations from the diaries reveal that some of the participants had unusual or special reasons for being interested in taking part in research on viewing. One man, for example, was regularly exchanging video diaries with several people around Europe. The researchers did not ask for information on ethnic background, and so are unable to discuss how ethnicity is related to television viewing. Nevertheless, this research is on a much larger scale than the earlier ethnographic audience studies, and its findings (for example, on use of remote-controls by gender) can be taken as authoritative.

Longitudinal studies that involve a panel of respondents face the problem of maintaining the involvement of the participants over the period of the research. Some participants will die, others will move (perhaps without telling the researchers their new address) and yet others may lose interest and not wish to continue. This problem is known as 'sample attrition'.

QUESTIONS

KNOWLEDGE AND UNDERSTANDING

1 In what 1988 project did this research have its origins?
2 What significant event for broadcasting occurred between 1988 and the start of this research?
3 What were respondents asked to do in addition to responding to the diary questions?
4 What is meant by 'sample attrition'?
5 What can be done to reduce sample attrition?
6 What differences did the research find between television viewing by elderly and retired people and by people who were younger?
7 Which aspects of the research are not usually seen as 'ethnographic'?

ANALYSIS

1 Evaluate the usefulness of longitudinal research.
2 Evaluate the usefulness of (a) a conventional questionnaire and (b) unstructured interviews in people's homes as methods of studying television viewing within families.
3 How might multi-channel television change viewing practices, and how could this be researched?

References   Ang, I (1985), *Watching Dallas*, Methuen, London
Morley, D (1986), *Family Television*, Comedia, London

DEAR BBC:
CHILDREN, TELEVISION STORYTELLING AND THE PUBLIC SPHERE

Maire Messenger Davies

Cambridge University Press, Cambridge, 2001

CONTEXT

This book reports on the findings of research carried out in 1996–97 assessing children's responses to televised storytelling, including both children's television and adult programmes watched by children.

The research was concerned specifically with programmes broadcast by the BBC and was designed to inform BBC policies. The BBC was set up to be a provider of public-service broadcasting, at first by radio and then television. Until the 1990s, its position as a public-service broadcaster meant that it was not subject to market forces. Its position and future were guaranteed by a public charter, and the television licence fee (paid by everyone owning a television) gave it financial security.

However, in the 1990s technological developments (such as satellite and cable television) and new political ideas favouring the extension of the free market into previously protected areas, combined to put new pressures on the BBC. The greater choice available to television audiences – and the certainty of even greater choice when digital television arrived – led the BBC to look again at its position and its services. The BBC's new competitors attacked the unfair advantage, as they saw it, that the BBC's financing through the licence fee and its protected position gave it.

In the area of children's television, governments had always regulated the services provided – for example, requiring ITV channels to allocate a minimum amount of air time to programmes aimed specifically at children and to ensure that those programmes reached a certain standard of quality. The requirements of public-service broadcasting had led to accusations that the BBC was too paternalistic in its children's programming. Others saw quality (and the commitment to education as well as entertainment) under threat. What would happen to children's television in the era of multi-channel television, with the arrival of children's channels dominated by American cartoons? BBC's share of the 4–15-year-old television audience fell from 44% to 35% between 1991 and 1995. Over the same period, satellite television's share (through children's channels such as Nickelodeon, the Children's Channel, Cartoon Network and Disney as well as 'adult' channels such as Sky 1 and the Movie Channel) had risen from 7 to 15%.

A second context for the research is the continuing debate over the importance and effects of television, both in general and for children in particular. As the ownership of television spread in the mid-1950s, Richard Hoggart (1958) and others argued that it had harmful effects on popular culture. The supposed passivity of viewers was seen as an important part of this, with people (the working class in Hoggart's arguments) staying at home rather than getting involved in local community life, which then lost its cohesion and vitality. The early media, such as the first newspapers, had been seen as helping to create a society in which information could be circulated and decision-making influenced by well-informed citizens. Television, however, was seen as a threat to that kind of society.

Research into the effects of the media has often been designed to prove harmful effects, usually in the form of violent behaviour. Such research is often based on psychology, with an emphasis on individual behaviour, and uses experimental methods that test short-term effects. In such research it is very difficult to control for the possible influence of social and other factors and to prove that violent or aggressive behaviour has been due to media influence rather than any other possible cause. Against this tradition of research has been another that is sceptical of claims about effects. This tradition, sometimes known as a 'cultural studies approach', emphasises the diversity of media audiences and the many ways audiences can respond. People are seen as making selective use of the media for their own purposes rather than being manipulated or misled into doing things they would otherwise not do. In other words, the audience control any effects the media will have on them.

In the case of children, there has been concern about violence, for example in cartoons, and about children being able to watch programmes showing violence or sexual behaviour or containing swearing. Underlying much of the concern have been assumptions that children are more easily influenced by television than adults, and that they need to be protected from some viewing content. An outcome of this in British terrestrial television has been the nine o'clock watershed, while films and videos have a classification system based on age groups. Such measures have often been considered ineffective. Neil Postman (1985), for example, has argued that television has ended the prolonged childhood of the period before the 1960s; television now makes children grow up more quickly.

A recent development in the sociology of childhood has been an increasing conviction that it is essential to consult children, to treat them fully as individuals. For researching children's television, the implications of this view are that it is necessary to provide children themselves with opportunities to contribute their views, and that it is important to understand how children see and think about television. Children have often been excluded from debates about children and childhood; this research was intended to redress this imbalance.

METHODS

A total of 1,276 children took part in the research, 631 boys and 645 girls. They were aged from six to twelve and were from 17 schools, all of which were mixed (boys and girls) and of mixed ability. At the schools' request, the researchers did not record data on ethnicity or socio-economic status. The decision to focus on younger children was taken because teenagers' voices are already heard quite regularly (as they are more confident and articulate). It is the views of younger children that are less likely to be sought and listened to. Older pupils were at secondary schools, younger ones at primary schools. The schools were chosen so that different groups of children would be represented; for example, there were inner London, outer London, inner-city non-London, outer-city non-London and rural schools.

The research used a standardised questionnaire that had been previously piloted. For younger children, a pictorial version was used and the researcher read out the questions. Questions covered children's views of television, including adult programmes, and questions about which programme (chosen from a list) respondents would choose to watch. The questionnaire also produced some qualitative data, because some questions allowed children to respond at length, or to respond by using drawings. The final question was, 'Is there anything else you would like to say about children's television?'

There were also discussion tasks which were carried out in fourteen schools but which did not, on the advice of the schools, involve under-eights. These tasks involved all the pupils in a class working on an educationally useful activity that did not disrupt their education. Tasks included, for example, groupwork on scheduling programmes from a list for a children's channel. Finally, the researchers carried out recorded one-to-one interviews with professional programme- and policy-makers.

KEY FINDINGS

Television was a natural and fully accepted part of the children's world. They were familiar with all of the programmes named in the questions. The children also found it natural that their views should be asked for, and responded positively – confident that their opinions would be listened to.

Over half the sample had a television in their bedroom, and 43% had access to satellite or cable television. For the question, 'Do you watch this channel?' Children's BBC had the greatest number of 'yes' responses (84%), followed by Children's ITV (68%). Cartoon Network did best of the non-terrestrial channels (47%). These figures were fairly constant as age increased (86% of seven-year-olds saying they watched CBBC and 84% of 12-year olds, for example). CBBC and CITV were just as strong amongst older as younger children. Gender differences were also slight; the researchers concluded that television was widely and equally used by both sexes.

Children's awareness of the arrival of multi-channel television showed in suggestions for having more channels. There was, however, a degree of scepticism about the service provided by multi-channel television ('there's no point, it's just repeats' said one boy of satellite film-channels). The children in the survey preferred BBC and ITV, occasionally watching satellite and cable channels.

In the television-scheduling exercises, children did not simply opt for commercial and down-market programmes such as *Mad for It*, but rather saw as a priority the provision of a variety of programmes appealing to different audiences. A group of 12-year-old boys in Cardiff put it this way:

> 'We came to a decision that we should put programmes for younger children, e.g. Fudge, first and then work up through the ages gradually and finishing with Top of the Pops, with Newsround in the middle because we think it's important for children to know what's going on in the world' (p4)

Children put forward the case for particular programmes by referring to the rights and needs of groups within the audience rather than popularity; in other words, children used the arguments of public-service broadcasting, rather than the market. The importance attached to the task, and their understanding of the issues, was highlighted when a group of media teachers were later asked to do the same exercise. Davies describes how the teachers, adopting the personae of young children, were unable to cooperate and failed to consider how to create a schedule for different groups. They assumed that the children would be socially irresponsible and think only of themselves.

The questions about the programmes children would choose raised concerns about the future of high-quality drama. The questions provided alternatives for situations in which there was a choice of two, three, five or ten channels, and were designed to see what effects the introduction of multi-channel television would have. Children were initially given a choice between *Byker Grove* and *Rugrats*, then with viewing choice extended to include a further eight options, all popular programmes at the time. *Byker Grove*, a realistic drama set in the North-East, would only have a small core of loyal viewers in a multi-channel environment, and it might be difficult to justify investing in it – although it would clearly help meet the recommendation in the United Nations Convention on the Rights of the Child to emphasise and reinforce local identities.

IMPORTANCE

This research makes an important point by its very nature, in treating young children as people with the right to express opinions that should be listened to. The research is successful in making this possible, allowing us to hear voices that are usually not taken as seriously. Moreover, what the children say disproves assumptions often made; children were well aware of the needs and rights of others in broadcasting, and considered it important to meet these. While there were factual and conceptual misunderstandings what is most striking about the book is how aware even young children are of the issues multi-channel television raises, and how thoughtful and democratic their responses are.

It is also significant in that it was commissioned by the BBC, and will be used to help shape the future of programming for children. In showing the value of high-quality drama to children, the findings strengthen the case for not abandoning the distinctiveness of public-service broadcasting for children by accepting the inevitability of the dominance of cartoons and other down-market programmes on multi-channel television.

EVALUATION

Researching children is difficult. Davies discusses several issues that arose in this project. There are difficulties in designing a substantial questionnaire that children will be both able and willing to complete. The positive response by children to the project suggests that the researchers were successful.

There is a further problem, however, with researching this age group. Children change and grow quickly; the researcher inevitably generalises about the respondents at times, when lots of six- and twelve-year-olds will be very different in their experiences, their preferences and their ability to express themselves. These differences show, for example, in the answers to the questions about programme choice; *Scooby Doo* was the most popular choice among five- and six-year-olds but not popular with eleven- and twelve-year-olds. Any generalisations about the respondents need to be treated with caution since they are likely to conceal such differences.

QUESTIONS

KNOWLEDGE AND UNDERSTANDING

1 What is meant by public-service broadcasting?
2 What changes began to affect public-service broadcasting in the 1990s?
3 How did this questionnaire produce some qualitative data?
4 Why did the research focus on six- to twelve-year-olds rather than teenagers?
5 In what ways did the researchers ensure that the youngest children could respond to the questions?
6 How, according to Postman, has television contributed to the disappearance of childhood?
7 Why does multi-channel television make it less likely that high-quality realistic children's dramas will be made?

ANALYSIS

1 What particular problems arise in constructing and carrying out a questionnaire with young children?
2 How can researchers try to achieve informed consent when working with children?
3 Is there a genre that we can call 'children's television?' Explain your answer.

References   Hoggart, R (1958), *The Uses of Literacy*, Penguin, Harmondsworth.
Postman, N (1985), *The Disappearance of Childhood*, Comet, London.

VIEWING THE WORLD:
A STUDY OF BRITISH TELEVISION COVERAGE OF DEVELOPING COUNTRIES

Department for International Development, 2000

CONTEXT

This research comprises three separate but related projects: a content study, an audience study and a production study. The first two of these were carried out by the Glasgow Media Group, and the third by 3WE (Third World and Environment Broadcasting Project). The research was commissioned by the Department for International Development to provide a detailed account of British television coverage of developing countries, which would inform policy in this area. This is therefore policy-oriented research, and contains recommendations for actions to be taken by broadcasting organisations, though not for government policy.

Previous research in this area has been mainly commissioned and published by the BBC and ITC, by development agencies such as UNICEF and Save the Children and by broadcasting pressure groups such as the Campaign for Quality Television. The commissioning and publication of research by the Department for International Development (the government department responsible for promoting development and the reduction of poverty in other countries) is therefore a significant departure. It reflects the greater commitment to international development expressed by the New Labour Government elected in 1997, the strengthening of the DFID and the increase in its budget.

Previous research has concentrated on content analysis of news and programming, and has suggested the existence of what has been called the 'coup–war–famine' syndrome, in which reporting is restricted to disasters and other negative news – leaving viewers uninformed about everyday life in the developing world.

The Glasgow Media Group has been well known since the publication in 1976 of *Bad News*, which documented how television news of industrial disputes was systematically biased in favour of the owners and managers of companies and against the employees who were taking action. This was followed by a series of studies also using the method of content analysis and demonstrating bias in different areas of news and documentary. From the late 1980s, the Glasgow Media Group has moved towards a greater interest in audiences and how they receive media messages and towards methods such as focus-group interviews. There has also been a move towards consideration of a wider range of media output, including reporting of the developing world. Previous Glasgow Media Group research on reporting of developing countries is described in two articles in the collection *Message Received* (1999), which is reviewed elsewhere in this book (on pp. 60–3).

3WE is a consortium of non-governmental agencies concerned with international development, environment and human-rights issues, including Oxfam, Save the Children and the Worldwide Fund for Nature. It was formed in 1989 and has published several research reports on global issues and the media.

METHODS

CONTENT STUDY (Glasgow Media Group)

The researchers analysed all main news programmes broadcast on networked terrestrial television channels in Britain (BBC1, BBC2, ITV, Channel Four and Channel 5) between 1 January and 31 March 1999. This was achieved by searching the BBC and ITN databases. A number of case studies of news stories were selected for detailed analysis as typical examples of the most frequent categories of news about developing countries; for example, the elections in Nigeria as an example of the reporting of politics. The researchers also analysed non-news output on these channels and on some cable and satellite channels in March 1999. Genres that had some coverage or mention of the developing world and that were studied included children's television, wildlife programmes, cookery programmes and Comic Relief.

AUDIENCE STUDY (Glasgow Media Group)

Focus groups were used to research how media messages about the developing world were received and understood by audiences. There were 26 focus groups, each consisting of six to eight people, involving a total of 165 people aged between ten and 74. The groups chosen were 'naturally occurring'; that is, they already knew each other through work, school, and family or friendship groups. Groups were given a series of exercises in which they either viewed and discussed programmes or sections of programmes, or looked at images from programmes and constructed their own news reports from these. The exercises were followed by group discussions focused on questions about development and television reporting of developing countries. The exercises and discussions were audio-taped and transcribed.

PRODUCTION STUDY (3WE)

This study involved asking policy- and programme-makers what coverage of the developing-world television should try to provide. Interviews were held with 38 people from the five British terrestrial television channels and from four satellite and cable channels. They were sampled from a range of levels in the programme-making hierarchy from Directors of Programmes and Channel Controllers to correspondents. Interviews lasted about one hour and were open-ended. Questions covered general programming trends, the criteria for commissioning programmes and factors that work for and against this area of programming.

KEY FINDINGS

CONTENT STUDY

The researchers defined 137 countries as developing and there was no discussion of, or reference to, 65 of these. A further 16 countries were only mentioned because of sports events, visits by Westerners, stories about animals, and the bizarre. It was found that there was most reporting of richer and more economically powerful countries (such as those in the Middle East and the bigger countries of the Pacific Rim) and a small number of countries with long-standing crises or natural disasters (such as civil war in Sierra Leone and an earthquake in Colombia). The main types of coverage were of conflict, sport, natural disasters and accidents, politics and visits by Westerners. These accounted for more than 80% of coverage. *Channel Four News* had more stories on the developing world than other programmes, while *Channel Four News* and *Newsnight* (BBC2) were the most likely to cover stories beyond the normal limited and usually negative reporting of disasters, conflicts and Western visitors. Other news programmes offered more limited reporting of the developing world.

AUDIENCE STUDY

About 25% of the sample said they had no interest at all in development issues while about 10% had an active interest. Perceptions of the developing world drawn from the media were mainly negative, with individual exceptions where people had direct experience of particular countries. Group members often recognised that they had a low level of understanding and that this was related to the quality of television coverage. Some made suggestions for improved coverage: that people in developing countries should be seen as actively helping themselves; that there should be more about the everyday rather than the strange and exotic, and that rebuilding and reconstruction after disasters should be reported.

There were differences between focus groups related to age, income, geographical location and ethnic origin. For example, the 15-year-olds had little interest or understanding, while the ten-year-olds showed more interest and some wanted more information.

PRODUCTION STUDY

The researchers found a strong belief that, even in the new world of multi-channel television, mainstream television has a role to play in informing people about the developing world. All the interviewees felt that there was a place for such coverage on their own channels. However, this kind of output is now regarded as a problem area because the respondents believed that the public do not want such programmes. In the past, programmes about the developing world could be made because public-service broadcasting valued the subject regardless of mass-audience interest. Multi-channel television has given more power to audiences, and channels now have to win audiences to justify their existence.

The respondents still held strongly to the public-service broadcasting ethos and felt their channels ought to provide better coverage but faced problems about what audiences wanted. There was, however, a feeling that innovative ideas could lead to programming that reported the links between the lives of people in Britain and in the developing world in ways that attracted viewers.

IMPORTANCE

The importance of this study lies in its thoroughness and authoritativeness, and in the presentation together of findings from three different studies, making possible an overview of this area.

There are no great surprises in the findings; the content analysis essentially confirms the finding from earlier research that the developing world is under-reported, and that what reporting there is concentrates on the negative. The audience study confirms that many people find most news and programmes about the developing world uninteresting, and that this contributes to the low level of understanding. The production study does add a new dimension to these findings, providing an insight into the conditions and pressures under which programming decisions are made.

The context of the report is also important. The public-service broadcasting age in which programmes about developing countries could be justified on the grounds of public interest even if they attracted few viewers has given way to the age of multi-channel television in which the old public-service broadcasters have to consider commercial pressures. One of the most interesting and significant findings is perhaps the extent to which those interviewed in the production study still believe in the importance of providing a public service.

EVALUATION

By covering three aspects of media – content, audience and production – this research provides an authoritative overview of television reporting of the developing world. It provides strong evidence confirming the view that news of the developing world tends to be negative, but is then able to consider both how audiences receive such messages and how producers and other media professionals view their work.

One problem with any study of news content over a period is whether the content can be assumed to be typical of content at other periods. The period of three months here is probably long enough to provide a picture of the types and distribution of news stories over time. The report does not, however, consider how particular news stories about Britain or the developed world might have affected coverage of the developing world by increasing or reducing the time that might be available or by arousing interest about particular types of news story.

The researchers used the BBC and ITN databases, which index all news output for commercial sale. As the report comments, 'This indicates that they are relatively reliable, but it doesn't guarantee that absolutely everything which is broadcast is properly catalogued or retrievable.'

Content analysis, because it produces quantitative data, might be assumed to have a high level of objectivity. In fact, decisions taken by researchers about what to measure and how to count or record instances mean by that the findings are shaped by judgements. In this case, for example, there were decisions about how to categorise coverage (sport, conflict, politics, trade, and so on) and then about how to allocate each news story to a particular category.

The use of focus groups for the audience study raises a number of difficulties. The Glasgow Media Group and others have increasingly used focus groups for media research. It is argued that people do not respond to the media as isolated individuals; their response is shaped also by discussion with others. In this case, both the construction of the exercises and the group discussions require considerable skill from the researchers. The moderator of a group discussion, for example, has to judge when and how to intervene to steer the discussion towards the questions to be answered, and to monitor participation (for example, being aware of the risk of one person dominating discussion so that the views of others who may disagree are not heard).

The production study used interviews with a sample of media professionals. Details are not provided of how the sample was selected or of whether any of those asked declined to take part. Some quantitative results are presented, but most of the results are in the form of a commentary supported by extensive use of quotation from the interviews. There is always a risk with this of researchers selecting material that coincides with their own opinions or that is particularly well expressed, rather than presenting a full range of opinions.

QUESTIONS

KNOWLEDGE AND UNDERSTANDING

1. What were the three studies undertaken within this research project?
2. Approximately what percentage of developing countries was not mentioned at all on British terrestrial television during the period of the research?
3. What two types of developing country were the most likely to be reported on?
4. Which channel's news programme had the most news about developing countries?
5. Name three genres of programme, other than news and documentary, in which there may be coverage of developing countries.
6. What is meant by a 'naturally occurring' focus group?
7. What is meant by a 'production study'?

ANALYSIS

1. Evaluate the extent to which content analysis can be seen as an objective method of gathering data.
2. Evaluate the usefulness of focus groups in researching how audiences receive media messages.
3. Do you think that a public-service broadcasting ethos survive in the age of multi-channel television? Explain the reasons for your view. What are the implications of your view for the reporting of less-developed countries?

References Glasgow University Media Group, (1976), *Bad News*, Routledge, London

Philo, G (ed.), (1999), *Message Received*, Addison Wesley Longman, Harlow

MESSAGE RECEIVED:
GLASGOW MEDIA GROUP RESEARCH 1993–1998

Edited by Greg Philo

Addison Wesley Longman, Harlow, 1999

CONTEXT

This book brings together the key research findings from the Glasgow Media Group (named because of their location at Glasgow University) in the 1990s. The research considers the production, content and reception of media messages by audiences. The studies were conducted by different members of the group but share common themes and methods. They cover a range of issues related to the media, from reporting news from Africa to soap operas and representations of race. Most studies are concerned with television but some also cover film and newspapers.

The Glasgow Media Group have been influential in the sociology of the mass media since the 1970s. Their early work, such as *Bad News* (1976) and *More Bad News* (1980) broke new ground in analysing television news reporting using content analysis.

The Glasgow Media Group's most recent research has different emphases from the earlier research. The present volume is concerned both with how audiences make sense of media messages and with the content of the message. The interest in audiences began with *Seeing and Believing* (1990) and is further developed here.

The Group have responded to changes in the media, in society more widely and in media studies.

THE MEDIA CONTEXT
The Glasgow Media Group's earlier research was carried out when broadcasting was dominated by the public sector and when there were a limited number of free channels which were aimed at national audiences. Today, the media are, with some exceptions, owned and controlled by global-media corporations who produce an almost limitless number of channels, dedicated to particular genres (such as sport or film) to increasingly segmented audiences who pay the provider.

THE SOCIAL CONTEXT
These changes in the mass media are closely related to wider social changes arising from the dominance of the Conservative Party and of New Right ideology in the 1980s and 1990s. The attack on public-service broadcasting was part of a wider assault on the public sector – opening up more areas of social life to the market, and widening inequalities.

THE MEDIA SOCIOLOGY CONTEXT
Philo is very critical of the trend within media studies towards emphasising how media texts (such as television programmes) can be interpreted in many ways by different audiences. This approach tends to assume that the media cannot have powerful effects (since audiences determine the meanings). Thus, for example, some writers have forcefully rejected the idea that violence in the media can influence people to be more violent. The research collected here presents strong evidence that

the media can, in fact, have powerful effects. This book therefore represents a significant intervention in a long-running debate, with Philo being strongly critical of those who claim audiences are all-powerful. Elsewhere, Philo and Miller (2000) have argued that most media and cultural studies research fails to be critical or to engage with public issues; it is a form of 'cultural compliance'. The research in this book aims to rescue media studies from postmodernists and insists on the importance of a critical understanding of the media.

METHODS

Three research projects from the book have been selected here to give an impression of the general approach adopted by the Glasgow Media Group and the specific methods used.

CHILDREN AND FILM/VIDEO/TV VIOLENCE by Greg Philo

This research investigated the reactions of children to *Pulp Fiction*, a film known for its violent content and cult status. Ten children from a comprehensive school in Glasgow were interviewed. Five of the children were interviewed as a group, two as a pair and the other three individually. They were asked a series of open questions focusing on who they saw as 'cool' or 'uncool' in the film. The children were also shown four photographs of two scenes from the film and asked to write the script accompanying the film. This enabled the researchers to assess the children's ability to remember the film, so they could judge the impression it had on them.

'JUST ANOTHER FOOD SCARE?' PUBLIC UNDERSTANDING AND THE BSE CRISIS by Jacqui Reilly

This research investigated audience understandings of the issue of BSE, both before and after official acknowledgement of the seriousness of the risk, to assess how the media shaped audience perceptions. The research used focus groups that were based on 'pre-existing' groups (that is, people who already knew each other as friends, neighbours, workmates, and so on) rather than being strangers to each other. The groups selected were diverse, including both those who might be expected to have a knowledge of food safety, such as restaurant staff and health-promotion professionals, and those might have no such knowledge, such as university students and art-gallery administrators.

THE MEDIA AND THE RWANDA CRISIS: EFFECTS ON AUDIENCES AND PUBLIC POLICY by Greg Philo, Lindsey Hilsum, Liza Beattie and Rick Holliman

This research investigated the quality of the information available to those who watched television reports of the Rwandan refugee crisis in July 1994. It follows from earlier Glasgow Media Group studies of reporting on Third World issues, such as the media response to the Ethiopian famine of 1984–85. It also considers how television reporting may have affected responses to the crisis by governments and non-governmental agencies. The researchers describe their method as thematic analysis, consisting of 'a detailed examination of the language and visuals of a sequence of news reports across all the main television channels'. The method aims to uncover key themes in the reporting and to show how these themes then decide how stories are reported and developed. It includes counting the number of times a theme is referred to. The researchers also interviewed press officers, journalists and staff of non-governmental agencies.

KEY FINDINGS

In different ways, the research projects here show that the media can have a powerful impact on audiences.

1. Although children (and adults) can distinguish fiction and reality in the media, this does not mean that the media do not have effects. The media provide models for their audiences; in the case of *Pulp Fiction*, it was clear that most children went along with the idea that violence could be 'cool'. While there are many influences on behaviour other than the media, Philo argues that this idea is not being effectively challenged – in the media or elsewhere.
2. The ability of the media to influence beliefs and actions is confirmed by other research in the book. Media reporting of the BSE crisis in 1996 caused a number of changes among the members of the focus groups. Respondents reported a sense of shock and even outrage that the earlier reassurances were now admitted to be wrong, and some said that they had made changes to their consumption patterns – for example, by stopping eating beef.
3. In the case of the Rwanda crisis, the media's distorted reporting led to a lack of action by governments. The reporting concentrated on the refugee crisis rather than the genocide that preceded it. The media failed to put pressure on governments to halt the genocide, then failed to explain how the genocide led to the refugee crisis. Audiences were not helped to understand the situation; they saw only the apparently worthy attempts to help the refugees rather than the failure to protect the victims of the genocide. The knowledge that actions will be reported by the media also has effects. In the case of Rwanda, aid programmes were designed to gain the best media coverage, regardless of the extent to which this helped the refugees.

The research on audiences shows the complex processes by which audiences make sense of the media. Audiences are well aware of the nature of media reporting and make judgements about the reliability of sources and content. Some respondents, for example, dismissed the reports of a link between BSE and its human equivalent, CJD, as a media scare. Audiences sometimes accept what they are told, and at other times do not.

These research findings and other have led the Glasgow Media Group to develop a model that they term 'the circuit of mass communications'. The three phases of the process of communication are: production, content and audience reception. The reception of messages by audiences is one part of this continuous process.

While firmly believing that they have demonstrated the importance of media effects, the Glasgow Media Group do not claim to provide answers to all the questions about media effects. They believe that the exact nature of influence varies in different circumstances, and there is therefore a need continually to examine the content of the mass media and its reception by audiences. This means empirical research, as in this book, rather than producing grand theories.

The aspect of this book that has proved controversial is the claim that the media can have powerful effects. For many, any such argument is associated with the 'hypodermic syringe' model, or is seen as a way of scapegoating the media when the real problems lie elsewhere. The conventional left-wing argument has been that by, say, blaming television and videos for violent behaviour, governments could avoid tackling structural problems in society such as unemployment, poverty and the breakdown of communities that create a situation in which violence became a more likely response to problems.

IMPORTANCE

The Glasgow Media Group believes their research shows clearly that the media can have powerful effects on attitudes and behaviour. It is very difficult to prove such claims, however, because there are so many possible influences on attitudes and behaviour. Moreover, the group's research shows that different audiences react in different ways, which seems to suggest that the media cannot easily be used to produce particular effects. Perhaps for this reason, the Glasgow Media Group no longer use terms associated with Marxism such as 'dominant ideology'. However, this book contains a clear political agenda; it is a book deeply committed to influencing social and media policy as well as encouraging a more critical attitude to the media. Philo argues that the media often accept as uncontested facts assumptions based on New Right ideology.

EVALUATION

A number of critical points can also be raised about the specific research projects. Some of these points are discussed in the book and do not have easy solutions.

1. The selection of respondents and focus groups is not representative (nor is it claimed to be). The research on children's responses to *Pulp Fiction*, for example, involved a very small sample – ten twelve-year-olds in one school. Research in other schools or with different age children might have yielded different results.
2. Involving people in interviews may have the effect of producing attitudes that do not really exist. For example, the focus groups that discussed BSE in 1992–93 may have been made more interested in (or sensitive to) such issues by being involved in group discussions, and their later discussion may then not be valid.
3. Thematic analysis produces both quantitative and qualitative data. Both involve a degree of personal judgement. A different researcher can reach a different decision about what the themes are, or about whether a particular item should count as a reference to that theme.

QUESTIONS

KNOWLEDGE AND UNDERSTANDING

1. Name two books produced by the Glasgow Media Group before the book described here.
2. Identify two different methods used by the Glasgow Media Group in this book.
3. In what key way does the research in this book differ from that in the earlier work of the Glasgow Media Group?
4. In what ways did the presence of the media in the Rwanda crisis affect the behaviour of those providing aid?
5. What do Philo and Miller mean by 'cultural compliance'?
6. What are the three aspects of the circuit of mass communications?
7. What is meant by 'thematic analysis'?

ANALYSIS

1. What factors might influence the way in which audiences respond to news reports?
2. How important is the fact that participants in Glasgow Media Group research do not constitute representative samples?
3. Assess the arguments for and against the claim that it is possible to measure media effects on attitudes and behaviour.

References Miller, D and Philo, G (2000), *Market Killing*, Longman, Harlow
Philo, G (1990), *Seeing and Believing*, Routledge, London
University of Glasgow Media Group (1976), *Bad News*, Routledge, London
University of Glasgow Media Group (1980), *More Bad News*, Routledge, London

FROCK ROCK:
WOMEN PERFORMING POPULAR MUSIC

Mavis Bayton

Oxford University Press, Oxford, 1998

CONTEXT

The best-known studies of women as producers of popular media have concerned women as editors, journalists and workers in film and television. The area of popular music has been generally neglected. In this book, Mavis Bayton, a musician as well as a sociologist, describes the experiences of women in popular music. Very little academic work had previously been done on this topic, although interestingly Bayton found that a common response to her work was, 'not another book on women and rock'.

Bayton was able to draw on the work of Simon Frith who has written extensively about the sociology of rock and of youth culture. He has described how male music-journalists have a powerful influence as cultural intermediaries. They act as 'gatekeepers', able to make decisions about the success or failure of bands.

Bayton is a feminist and her work is clearly shaped by the work of feminist sociologists such as Ann Oakley, Sheila Rowbotham and Dale Spender. Her focus on women as producers of music, and on the dominance of men and of male ideology in the music industry, suggests a Marxist or socialist-feminist approach. She does not believe that the equal-rights legislation of the 1970s led to equality. Women remained segregated and discriminated against in work and girls lacked equal opportunities in the school. Women's progress was held back by the repressive social policies of the Conservative governments from 1979 onwards, and there was a 'backlash' (described by Susan Faludi in the book of that name (1992)) against the limited progress women had made.

By the time this book was published, it had become common to hear that women had made considerable progress towards equality and that feminism had become unnecessary, even counter-productive. In popular music, the success of the Spice Girls convinced many that women were equally represented, despite the fact that they did not play instruments. Another argument was that women could succeed if they wanted to – and if they would just stop complaining and get on with it. Bayton refutes these views, demonstrating the considerable obstacles in the way of women, and the slow pace of change.

METHODS

Bayton began researching this topic in the 1980s and intended publishing the results then as a book, but her partner became seriously ill and soon died. In order to ensure her book was up to date, Bayton then repeated the entire research in the mid-1990s.

Bayton's approach is ethnographic, involving informal interviews and participant observation. Bayton's 1980s research involved 49 interviews, most of them lasting more than two hours, with female musicians at different stages of their careers. She used an interview schedule of more than 200 questions. She also went to women's music workshops, carried out brief, informal unstructured interviews with men and women involved in music and attended hundreds of gigs. In 1995–96 she carried out a further 56 interviews. There were thus a total of 105 interviews. The 1980s interviews were confidential, so although Bayton provides a list of respondents in an appendix, many of the names are pseudonyms. The main focus of the research was on local, amateur or semi-professional rock music. However, some of the named respondents are well known (Skin from Skunk Anansie; Cerys Matthews, who used to be in Catatonia; Debbie Smith from Echobelly, for example). A number of famous women refused to be interviewed; Bayton explains that such people would receive several requests for interviews every day, mostly from journalists able to offer publicity. However, most of the women she approached were interested and supportive.

The majority of respondents played instruments in bands but others were, for example, vocalists, administrators or music teachers. Bayton collected information on career-stage, location, type of music played, instrument, age, sex, class and sexuality. Bayton deliberately included several 'older' respondents (in their 30s or 40s) and several from minority ethnic-groups, although there are relatively few musicians from these categories in rock/indie music.

Most of the interviews were conducted face to face, although a few were telephone conversations. They took place in settings as various as backstage, in pubs and cafés, recording studios, kitchens and bedrooms. They were all recorded. Bayton made the interviews as relaxed and friendly as possible and encouraged respondents to ask her questions as well.

Bayton also carried out surveys of the content of music media in both 1988 and 1996, such as radio programmes, the television programme *Top of the Pops*, charts and magazines including the music press (such as *New Musical Express*) and specialist trade magazines (such as *Guitarist*)

KEY FINDINGS

Women are a minority within all fields of activity in popular music; they are even outnumbered as vocalists. Very few women play drums, bass or electric guitar. Women are judged more by appearance than by musical ability. (Singing does not seem to count as musical ability in the music press; for example, female singers are rarely asked how they learnt their techniques).

Women face a wide range of factors that act as constraints on their involvement in music. Bayton does not attempt to put these in order because, she believes, they interact with and reinforce each other. They include: having less money than men; having less access to technical equipment; less mobility (for example, they are less likely to own a car); less private space; less time because of the pressure of domestic roles; restrictions imposed by parents (later by husbands or boyfriends); and being excluded by male musicians. The presence of girls (even as a girlfriend rather than a musician) is often seen by male band members as threatening a special male-bonding that holds bands together. Bayton also shows how girls are treated condescendingly in music shops and made to feel inferior and unwanted.

The result is that women who do succeed in music at any level have to be determined and have strength of character. They are, by definition, exceptional. Amongst the factors that helped them were: coming from a musical family; having classical music training; having an art education (attending an art school); involvement in drama; being at university (which provides escape from parental restrictions); having a musician boyfriend or husband; and having female role-models. With regard to the family, fathers were found to be significant as well as mothers – especially fathers who conformed to gender roles themselves but treated a daughter as if she were a boy.

Bayton's interviewees were often gender rebels, following 'male' subjects at school, riding motorbikes or having had 'masculine' jobs such as van driver, electrical engineer or plumber. This applied both in 1988 and 1996. Bayton argues that the confidence gained in childhood and adolescence from engaging in 'male' activities enabled them later to learn to play 'masculine instruments' and play in a male-dominated area of music.

There was a surge of women into music in the late 1970s due to punk rock and second-wave feminism. In 1995 some interviewees still mentioned the importance of punk, but by then feminism and lesbianism (which had been important earlier for many) no longer provided ways into music.

Female bands do not seem to form in the traditional way male bands do, through a group of friends in the same area (often at school or college together) gradually evolving into a band. Bayton describes the various stages involved in being a female rock band – from learning to play and write together to deciding what to wear on stage (some deliberately dress down in the hope of being taken seriously) to the problems of gigging and working with record companies.

The 1996 respondents had clearly been influenced by feminist ideas about equality. They expected to be treated equally and insisted on this. Nevertheless, Bayton argues, a long series of barriers remained in their way.

In her surveys of the music media, Bayton found that women were under-represented and that there was very little change between 1988 and 1996. For example, in 1996 the Top 40 album chart had no all-female bands and over half of the albums had no female presence at all. Bayton estimates that there were about six female instrumentalists featured on these albums, out of a total of between 80 and 100. Detailed results are also given for a range of different media, confirming that women rarely featured. In pop, as opposed to rock and indie music, there were even fewer women involved than in 1988. Music journalism remains dominated by male journalists.

IMPORTANCE

Within the sociology of mass media at A-level, popular music tends to be neglected, despite its central importance in the lives of many people, young and old. Bayton provides a comprehensive account of how men dominate in this area of cultural life – and of the many constraints, small and large, that hold women back. The despondency this may cause is, however, offset by the examples set by Bayton's respondents: women determined to succeed on their own terms in a male-dominated sphere. The use of quotations from respondents enables us to hear the experiences of women musicians in their own words. The result is a lively, entertaining book full of insights into the world of rock and indie music. It will, perhaps, not only inform sociology students but also inspire some female readers to learn to play instruments and form their own bands. After all, as Bayton concludes, 'Why should boys have all the fun?'

EVALUATION

The evidence Bayton presents is strongly persuasive, with the respondents allowed to express their thoughts and experiences directly to the reader. As with all such research using quotations from interviews within an ethnographic approach, there is a potential problem with generalisation. Statistics are provided on the music media, the charts, and so on, but not on the conclusions drawn from the interviews. The women musicians Bayton interviewed had a range of experiences and not all were held back by the constraints some of them describe. By concentrating on those who have succeeded or persevered, Bayton may perhaps even underestimate the obstacles women face in popular music. The voices of those women who gave up in despair are missing.

QUESTIONS

KNOWLEDGE AND UNDERSTANDING

1 'I am a white, heterosexual woman, a sociologist, a feminist, and a musician.' Why does Bayton feel it is important to describe herself as such to her readers?
2 What is meant by an 'interview schedule'?
3 Identify and explain four types of constraint on women musicians.
4 How might being at university or art college, rather than living at home, help women become musicians?
5 Name two settings in which Bayton carried out participant-observation research to support her interviews
6 In what way might fathers make it easier for daughters to become musicians?
7 What is meant by a 'gender rebel'?

ANALYSIS

1 Why do you think popular music has been neglected in media sociology, compared with print and broadcast media?
2 What parallels can be drawn between the situation of women musicians and of women in other media?
3 What problems might a male researcher have faced in researching women in popular music?

References Faludi, S (1992) Backlash: *The Undeclared War Against Women*, Chatto and Windus, London

CLUB CULTURES:
MUSIC, MEDIA AND SUBCULTURAL CAPITAL

Sarah Thornton

Polity Press, Cambridge, 1995

CONTEXT

The subject of this book, 'club cultures', refers to the youth cultures based first around raves and then around dance clubs from the late 1980s to the mid-1990s.

The main sociological context for Thornton's research was the approach to the study of youth subcultures developed in the 1970s by the Centre for Contemporary Cultural Studies at the University of Birmingham in books such as *Resistance Through Rituals*. This approach saw subcultures such as skinheads as expressions of class-based cultures that were rebelling against the dominant ideology of a capitalist state.

Throughout the 1960s and 1970s there were a series of what have been called 'spectacular' youth subcultures: mods, rockers, skinheads, punks, and so on. Every subculture had a distinctive style of dress and appearance and particular tastes in music and usually in choice of drugs. Many of these subcultures were analysed by sociologists along the lines suggested by the CCCS – that is, seen as representing a primitive kind of resistance towards capitalism.

From the 1980s onwards it became much more difficult to distinguish youth subcultures. Instead, there seemed to be a variety of styles that were short lived and shaped by the music and fashion industries. These could not be seen as authentic expressions of the anger of working-class youth in the way the CCCS had suggested. Thornton's research focuses on a subculture, or cluster of related subcultures, in the late 1980s and 1990s.

Thornton takes from Pierre Bourdieu the concept of 'cultural capital' and develops from it the concept of 'subcultural capital'. Bourdieu (1977) argued that the most privileged groups in society are distinguished by their possession not only of economic capital but also social and cultural capital, and that the class system is perpetuated by these various forms of capital (not just wealth) being passed from one generation to the next. Cultural capital in Britain, for example, might include possession of a particular accent, and having attended an independent rather than a state school. From this Thornton explores the idea that a subculture may also have forms of cultural capital (such as knowledge of the latest music) that give status within the subculture.

At the outset Thornton makes a series of points, derived from earlier findings but supported by her own, which establish the importance of club cultures.

- Admissions to clubs and other dance events are higher than those to sporting events, cinemas and 'live arts' combined; clubs only go relatively unnoticed because they concern only one particular age group and the activity is mainly after the rest of the population is in bed.
- There are few, if any, boundaries of class, race, ethnicity, gender and sexuality in dancing, but relatively firm lower- and upper-age boundaries. Young teenagers are excluded by parental rules about being out late and by lack of money, while older

clubbers lose interest as they leave home and enter cohabiting or marriage relationships.
- Clubbing is an integral part of growing up, providing a space where the young can act like adults in some ways and can achieve a distinct identity. Clubs are particularly empowering for girls. Dancing is the only out-of-home leisure activity that involves more females than males.
- Music is an essential aspect of youth cultures. Young people buy and listen to more music than any other age group

METHODS

Thornton used two main methods in her research.

1 Ethnographic research (participant observation and unstructured interviews) in which she went to raves and clubs and interviewed those involved in club cultures.
2 Secondary research involving the study of a wide range of sources both on club cultures and on earlier forms of youth culture.

Over four years Thornton was a participant observer at over 200 clubs, discos and raves and also attended at least 30 live gigs. She was therefore carrying out an ethnographic survey of dance cultures rather than a case study of one particular club or group of people. She was unable to find a way of constructing a random sample of clubs, and does not claim that the clubs she visited were a representative sample. She did, however, feel that she observed a very wide range of crowds, clubs and dancing styles; there was nothing that could be called 'typical', and the cultures were also in constant change.

One of the problems facing ethnographers is the relationship they have with the people they are studying. The nature of ethnographic research means that Thornton's background and values are important to evaluating her work. Thornton is Canadian, and came to Britain to research dance culture for her PhD. She says in the introduction that she had been an avid clubber. However, in studying British club cultures she felt herself an 'outsider', or as she puts it, 'a stranger in a strange land', for several reasons. She began her research at the age of twenty-three, but the research took several years, so that she became older than many of those she was studying. Her nationality was also important, because the kinds of youth cultures she describes are often localised (although the music can be global, the dance and style associated with it will vary between places). She was also working (doing her research) in places where almost everyone else was having a good time, and where the ethos of 'lose yourself in the music' opposed her commitment to research and analysis. These factors combined to make it possible for Thornton to keep a distance from her subject matter.

Thornton needed the help of members of the club cultures to carry out her research. She contacted people through the letters columns of the style magazines *The Face* and *iD* and the London listings magazines *City Limits* and *Time Out*. She used the replies she received to make contact with guides and informants, and as a source in themselves of information about the values of club culture.

Thornton's book contains extracts from her research diaries, describing visits to clubs on one night, Saturday 22 September 1990. The style of the description (in the present tense) suggests that it was written soon afterwards, based on memories still fresh. It is also clear that Thornton was asking questions as well as recording her impressions of the clubs. The extracts also tell us Thornton's answer to a problem faced by those doing ethnography with groups among whom drug use is normal: she shares a capsule of MDMA (ecstasy) with 'Kate', her companion and informant for the evening.

> 'I'm not a personal fan of drugs – I worry about my brain cells. But they're a fact of this youth culture so I submit myself to the experiment in the name of thorough research.' (p89)

Thornton's archival research covers a wide range of documents that she uses to describe the development of particular aspects of youth culture. For example, she uses the archives of the Musicians' Union to describe how the union, representing musicians who played in clubs and other places, responded to the threat to their livelihoods posed by the arrival of recorded music, and the musical press (*Melody Maker, New Musical Express, Billboard* and so on) to describe the evolution of the disc jockey.

KEY FINDINGS

Thornton reaches very different conclusions about club cultures from those that might have been reached by a researcher from the CCCS tradition.

SUBCULTURES

Popular culture is a space in which cultural differences are not about resistance to the power of the ruling class. Rather, groups create distinctions between themselves and others on the basis of subcultural capital. They acquire status within their own social world through possession of subcultural knowledge and through making distinctions between themselves and other groups of young people. This often involves a distinction between their own culture and that of the 'mainstream'. Thornton's respondents were contemptuous of the 'chartpop disco' where 'Sharon and Tracy dance around their handbags'. But this mainstream of 'them' doesn't really exist (after all, the charts are an eclectic mix of many kinds of niche music) and is defined simply as the opposite of 'us'.

ROLE OF THE MEDIA

The earlier tradition had assumed that subcultures began as authentic and subversive expressions of youth, then were taken over by the mass media and turned into commodities. Thornton argues that the media are implicated from the very beginning. Condemnation by the mass media is actively sought, while micro media (flyers, listings, fanzines, pirate radio, e-mail lists, and so on) are the sources of information that can supply subcultural capital. Clubbers produce these, and clubbers turn to them for information. Niche media (mainly the music and style consumer magazines) often try to identify and develop subcultures; *New Musical Express* was strongly associated first with punk and New Wave and later 'Madchester', while the established magazine that linked itself most closely to clubbing was *iD*. Subcultural capital relies on the media (but not mass media) which, in turn, means restricted accessibility. Subcultural capital is about 'being in the know'.

Thornton also notes how the media make use of sociological discourse and concepts in making sense of club cultures. They use terms like 'subculture' and 'moral panic'. This is an example of what Giddens (1991) has called, 'the reflexivity of modernity'.

IMPORTANCE

Thornton's approach to studying subcultures is very different from that of the Centre for Contemporary Cultural Studies in the following ways.

1 She regards empirical research as more important than the elaboration of theory.
2 She regards the mass media and popular-culture industries as inextricably bound up with cultures (for the CCCS, subcultures were constantly trying to avoid being incorporated, swallowed up and effectively neutralised).
3 She is concerned with social changes, particularly how club cultures were constantly changing
4 She treats the knowledge and values of club cultures as subcultural ideologies, as ways in which young people assert their differences from the mainstream.

By adopting this approach, Thornton gives an account of contemporary subcultures that readers are likely to find more convincing and relevant than earlier studies. This book should provide a wide range of ideas for further research.

EVALUATION

Thornton's book provides a wealth of information and ideas on popular music and dance cultures and subcultures. Her own primary research is personal, immediate and very readable. Her analysis of the media, with the useful distinction between micro media, niche media and mass media, and her history of dance music with the accolade of authenticity contested by live and recorded music, are also very informative. To all of this she brings an illuminating theoretical analysis, though here the reading may become challenging for A-level students.

In considering Thornton's ethnographic research, we need to be aware of the inevitable issues raised by such methods. Her findings will have been shaped by her age, gender and nationality and people's responses to these, her selection of 'guides', her recording of data (when and how notes were made), how she dealt with issues such as drug taking, and so on. As will all ethnographic research, these do not invalidate the findings but need to be borne in mind when assessing them.

KNOWLEDGE AND UNDERSTANDING

1 Why were the youth subcultures of the 1960s and 1970s sometimes referred to as 'spectacular'?
2 With which sociologist is the term 'cultural capital' associated?
3 How does subcultural capital differ from cultural capital?
4 Why is dancing in clubs particularly important for girls?
5 What is meant by ethnography?
6 What are micro media?

QUESTIONS

ANALYSIS

1 What problems might a researcher face in carrying out ethnographic research on subcultures?
2 To what extent do you think the facts that Thornton is (a) female and (b) Canadian affected this study?
3 Compare and contrast Thornton's approach to studying subcultures with that of the Centre for Contemporary Cultural Studies.
4 How useful is the concept of 'subcultural capital' to an understanding of club cultures?

References Bourdieu, P and Passeron, J-C (1977), *Reproduction in Education, Society and Culture*, Sage, London

Giddens, A (1991), *Modernity and Self-Identity: Self and Society in the Late Modern Age*, Polity Press, Cambridge

Hall, S and Jefferson, T (eds) (1976), *Resistance Through Rituals*, Hutchinson, London

CLUBBING:
DANCING, ECSTASY AND VITALITY

Ben Malbon

Routledge, London, 1999

CONTEXT

This book appears in a series titled *Critical Geographies*. The geographical basis of the book shows in references to the spaces and places of clubbing, but the main focus is on human behaviour in those spaces and places. Malbon cites sociologists and sociological concepts prominently among his influences, and both his subject matter and methodology are sociological. Thus, despite being nominally geography, this is a book worthy of attention from sociology students.

Sociological interest in the leisure activities of young people began with work within the Sociology Department at the University of Chicago in the early twentieth century. This led to a sociology of youth that was primarily concerned with youth as predominantly urban and as at least potentially deviant – a source of trouble. There was also a concentration on social interaction based on ethnographic methods and especially participant observation.

In Britain in the 1970s and 1980s the study of young people was developed further by sociologists at the Centre for Contemporary Cultural Studies (CCCS) at Birmingham University. The approach adopted here was neo-Marxist and particularly interested in what were seen as working-class youth subcultures expressing resistance against the dominant capitalist ideology. It drew on semiology to interpret the meaning of the styles young people adopted and on neo-Marxist social theorists. This approach came under criticism from about 1980 onwards. Amongst the points of criticism were:

- the assumption that youth subcultures were in some way subversive
- the assumption that youth subcultures could be seen as expressing, in a primitive way, working-class resentment towards the capitalist system – even when the victims of aggression were also working class (as in skinheads beating up Asian youths)
- the 'gap' between how young people talked about their subcultures and the sociological view of them
- the lack of attention paid to 'normal' young people rather than the 'spectacular' subcultures
- the lack of attention paid to girls.

By the 1990s sociologists were developing new ways of understanding youth subcultures, taking into account the criticisms above. This involved even rethinking the term 'youth subcultures' since although it seemed that most young people now belonged to a style-grouping these groups seemed in many ways unlike the earlier spectacular subcultures of mods, rockers, skinheads, punks, and so on. For example, young people's styles were partly expressed through a range of media and other industries. It was no longer the case, if it ever had been, that the establishment responded to a youth subculture by labelling its members as 'folk devils'.

The most thorough and influential study of young people's styles in Britain in the 1990s has been Sarah Thornton's *Club Cultures* (see pp. 68–71). Clubbing has become a very important leisure activity for many young people. It cannot really be described as a subculture, however, because it consists of many different styles and even sub-styles. Malbon writes approvingly of Thornton, but points out that she does not actually describe in any detail what the experience of clubbing is like and what it means to clubbers. He aims to address this using ethnographic methods, thus returning to the tradition established by the Chicago School.

Malbon also cites as an important influence on his work the French sociologist Michel Maffesoli (1996), in particular his concept of sociality and its importance in understanding the behaviour of crowds (in this case, the behaviour of young people in clubs). Malbon says, 'The practices that comprise sociality consist of ways of dressing, spoken and unspoken language, traditions and customs, myths and folklore, and the sharing of styles, knowledge and passions' (p25). Sociality holds social life together, for example, making it possible for people very different in age, class, ethnicity, gender and other ways to share an experience such as shopping together on the high street or in a shopping centre. Where functionalists emphasised norms and rules, Malbon and Maffesoli see social life in crowds as more about feelings and the present moment, constantly changing and negotiated.

This leads to a second major concept in Malbon's approach to clubbing, performativity. This refers to the two-way process in which people negotiate their membership of a crowd and their position within the crowd. Here Malbon is drawing on the work of Erving Goffman and, more recently, Judith Butler, on performance management. Clubbers are not passive consumers, they are social actors, and even getting admitted to a club requires competence in projecting a particular impression based on a knowledge of subtle distinctions of style and taste.

METHODS

When starting his research, Malbon had to decide what kind of clubs and clubbing to focus on. He decided to adopt a relatively narrow definition of clubbing, concentrating on what he saw as the largest general group of clubbers. The choice of the clubs visited with respondents was made by respondents themselves, but Malbon did try to ensure that he included the various sub-genres of clubs.

Malbon found his sample through letters printed in two style magazines, *The Face* and *iD*, and through two internet discussion groups. He received over 40 offers of help, and over a period of a year went clubbing with and interviewed 18 clubbers. He had some responses from other countries but selected those who lived in or near London or went clubbing in London. He tried to achieve an equal relationship with his respondents, emphasising that he was a clubber himself so as not to be taken as an 'outsider'.

Clubbers were interviewed twice, informally and without an interview schedule although all interviews were recorded. The first interview took place before Malbon went clubbing with a respondent, the purpose being: to put the clubber at ease, explain the purpose and nature of the research, find out something about the clubber as a clubber and to help Malbon plan how to approach the night out with the clubber. After spending at least one evening together clubbing a second interview took place, in which the clubber discussed the club visit. Malbon also encouraged interviewees to talk about their lives more widely, including hopes and plans for the future. Malbon describes almost all his respondents as being, 'unbelievably helpful.'

In addition to the interviews, Malbon kept a research diary describing the nights out. There are several extracts from this diary throughout the book.

KEY FINDINGS

A main reason clubbers go clubbing is because they can identify with the crowd at clubs and feel a sense of belonging, even though they are surrounded by people they wouldn't even notice outside the club. This can produce a sense of liberation, especially for women. Women are objects of sexual attention in settings such as pubs, but this is less so in clubs. Some women choose to look as sexually attractive as possible in clubs, but this is as much to please themselves as to please men.

The sense of belonging that seems to be a large part of many people's enjoyment of clubbing is closely related to ideas about being cool and trendy. This covers such things as styles of dress and speech, of dancing, choice of drink, clubbing venue and drugs. Cool is defined in relation to the mainstream. One clubber interviewed wanted to find himself among a crowd of people whom he and others took to be cooler than him, he was much less interested in the music and the DJ. Clubbers are concerned with how others perceive them, and part of this is who others see them with and where. Clubbers strive to belong. The final test is negotiating entry into the desired club; refusal can be traumatic.

The central experience of clubbing is dancing. By dancing, clubbers can both express individuality, feeling conscious of themselves as individuals, and can feel a sense of being part of the crowd that is experiencing the music. Dancing involves use of space, shaped by the music. Clubs are divided into areas for different activities (the bar, dance floor, toilets, etc.) and clubbers move between these, sometimes colonising areas and negotiating the use of space with others. These 'spacings' change constantly through the evening as the crowd changes in size, constitution and drug use, and as the music changes.

The experience of dancing in clubs is marked for many by feelings of joy, euphoria and a sense of release and escape, though often only for fleeting moments. This feeling of an 'altered state' is the main appeal of dancing. Malbon describes these feelings as 'oceanic experiences'. They are often, though not always, based on the use of recreational drugs such as ecstasy (MDMA). Drugs are used to trigger, prolong or intensify an oceanic experience. There are complex rituals about taking drugs.

Malbon does not interpret clubbing as in any way expressing resistance to a dominant culture. However, he does see the pursuit of 'playful vitality' as partly an escape from other aspects of the clubber's life, such as their work.

IMPORTANCE

Malbon adds considerably to our understanding of clubbing, which is important both as a leisure activity for many young people and as the equivalent today of the youth subcultures, the study of which still dominates this field. His ethnographic approach allows clubbers themselves to express their thoughts and feelings about what they do and why. His attention to the actual experience of clubbing and his structuring of the book so as to take us through the stages of a night out provides a focus for studying clubbing that adds significantly to the earlier work of Thornton (1995) in *Club Cultures*.

EVALUATION

As is always the case with ethnographic research, questions can be raised about the extent to which the findings can be taken as representative. Malbon used a small, self-selected sample of clubbers, and his study is specifically about clubbing in London. There is no way of knowing whether, or in what sense, his respondents might be typical. The data produced is qualitative; he does not attempt to provide statistics on, for example, the numbers of nights spent clubbing per week or amount of money spent per night by his respondents. His interest is rather in the experience of clubbing in terms of feelings, identifying with crowds and 'oceanic experiences'. The advantage of the approach taken is in allowing us to hear what clubbers themselves have to say, guided by sensitive questioning.

Malbon himself is a clubber, and his own experiences provided the starting point for his project. Such personal interest is in many ways valuable, but clearly Malbon will have produced a different account – emphasising the value of clubbing to clubbers – than an outsider would have. Because of the extensive use of illegal drugs by clubbers, the research did involve ethical issues. The names of respondents have, of course, been changed.

QUESTIONS

KNOWLEDGE AND UNDERSTANDING

1. Which discipline other than sociology strongly influenced this research?
2. How did Malbon make contact with his respondents?
3. What three methods did Malbon use?
4. Why did Malbon interview each respondent twice?
5. What is meant by 'sociality'?
6. What is meant by 'oceanic experiences'?

ANALYSIS

1. What are the advantages and disadvantages of the method Malbon used to find respondents?
2. What other activities and practices, perhaps in other cultures, do you know of that involve 'oceanic experiences'? In what ways are these different from or similar to clubbing?
3. Compare the account of clubbing given by Malbon to the work of earlier sociologists on youth subcultures.
4. Design a research tool for obtaining quantitative data about clubbing. In what ways would the data you obtained add to Malbon's account of clubbing?

References Butler, J (1997), *Excitable Speech :a Politics of the Performative*, Routledge, New York
Goffman, E (1971), *The Presentation of the Self in Everyday Life*, Penguin, Hardmondsworth
Maffesoli, M. (1996), *The Time of the Tribes: The Decline of Individualism in Mass Society*, Sage, London
Thornton, S (1995), *Club Cultures*, Polity Press, Cambridge

INSIDE SUBCULTURE:
THE POSTMODERN MEANING OF STYLE

David Muggleton

Berg, Oxford, 2000

CONTEXT

Inevitably, because this is a study of youth subcultures, the main sociological context of this book is provided by the writings and theories about subculture that came from writers associated with the Centre for Contemporary Cultural Studies (CCCS) at the University of Birmingham in the 1970s. Muggleton lists four books that he refers to as 'the CCCS approach'. These are *Resistance Through Rituals* by Hall and Jefferson (1976); *Working Class Youth Culture* by Mungham and Pearson (1978); *Profane Culture* by Willis and *Subculture: The Meaning of Style* by Hebdidge (1979).

Muggleton argues that this approach was flawed in several ways.

- It failed to consider the subjective viewpoint of the members of youth subcultures themselves, who would not recognise themselves in sociological accounts.
- There was a reliance on theory and analysis of style rather than on research involving members of youth subcultures.
- The theory was abstract and determinist, reading all working-class youth subcultures as embodying resistance to capitalist hegemony.
- The idea that subcultures had an existence of their own, created by and in opposition to capitalism, and independent of their members, was mistaken.

In opposition to this approach, Muggleton develops his own, which he refers to as neo-Weberian. He takes from Weber the idea that it is important to recognise the subjective meanings given to their actions by social actors. For his research, this means allowing members of subcultures to explain in their own way what the subculture and its style mean to them.

Muggleton's critical approach to the CCCS studies leads him also to ask questions about the youth subcultures of the 1960s and 1970s. He finds evidence that individuals moved between subcultures and that many styles that might have been defined as subcultures were never actually described, analysed and labelled. The situation was much more fluid and characterised by changing choices than the CCCS studies (which can even be said to have created the subcultures they described, because the act of description gave them a permanence) imply.

Muggleton is also concerned with how the subcultural styles he studies can be related to the idea that we now live in a postmodern world. In a postmodern world, he argues, we find the post-subculturalist. Drawing on work such as Widdicombe and Wooffitt's *The Language of Youth Subcultures* (1995), he hypothesises about post-subculturalists. There is no longer any sense of authenticity about subcultural styles, rather they involve constant borrowing and mixing, creating new hybrids. Post-subculturalists can engage in 'style-surfing', moving quickly and freely from one style to another. These and related hypotheses are then tested against the data provided by the interviews.

METHODS

Muggleton's main method was semi-structured interviews. He interviewed a total of 57 people, of whom 14 were female, in 38 separate interviews in 1994 and 1995. The age range was from 16 to 34, and the average age was 24. He selected his sample simply by approaching people whose appearance he regarded as making them suitable. The majority of the interviews were in Brighton, except for three which were in Preston. He also interviewed four young people, two male and two female, who were not members of subcultures (or as he puts it, were not subcultural); these acted as a control group, but their interviews are not discussed in this book. Over half of the sample were in casual or part-time work or were unemployed.

The interviews were informal, taking place in pubs and clubs – which were the places in which Muggleton usually approached potential respondents. He used an interview schedule, but in a flexible way, not always keeping to the order or wording of the questions. The importance of the questions was to act as prompts for discussion. He was willing to follow up promising lines of inquiry suggested by his respondents. He also revised the questions as seemed appropriate after interviews. The interviews took between 20 minutes and an hour and a half, the typical time being about 40 minutes, and all were taped and transcribed.

The interview schedule began by asking about age, current and previous work (if any) and parental background. Muggleton then asked how the respondent would describe themselves, how they chose their style, influences on them, and so on. Here is a sample sequence of questions from the schedule:

> 'Is it important to you to feel that you have your own, unique, individual way of dressing?
> What's being a [whatever] all about?/What's dressing in this style all about?
> Are you trying to say anything by wearing this style?/Can you tell me what it means to you?
> Do people who dress in this way tend to have anything in common apart from the style?
> Is this true for you personally?
> So what's the difference between people who dress like you and people who dress more conventionally?"
> (pp172–173)

KEY FINDINGS

Subculturalists do not regard themselves as members of fixed subcultural groups. For example, a respondent who described himself as a punk went on to define punk in terms of being an individual ('freedom, doing what you wanna do') rather than in terms of conforming to a style. The subculturalists either rejected all labels or accepted only those they could interpret widely, while stressing how they did not conform to any norm for that style. Respondents often referred to 'crossover' between different styles, creating groups that are very loose and without clear boundaries. They did not want to feel they belonged to any group because this implied a loss of individuality.

Subculturalists regularly cross boundaries between subcultural styles and between subcultural style and conventional style. Their attachment to any one style is therefore weak. Aspects of conventional style are borrowed and combined with subcultural aspects to create a new and individual style; this is known as bricolage. The subculturalist can wear the same item as conventional people, yet not be conventional.

All this does not mean that subculture is only about surface and image. Muggleton's respondents tended to look down on 'part-timers', who are only superficially members. A part-timer 'does' punk, but this is not the same as 'being' punk, which implies being a real, genuine punk. Thus, moving too quickly between styles – style-surfing – can mean being seen as being superficial and inauthentic.

There is a commitment to a style, but too strong a commitment was also seen as indicating a lack of authenticity.

Movement between styles is often gradual and seen as natural by the respondent. It is the respondent's own self-conception that counts, for labels applied by others can be rejected as based only on appearance (such as a hairstyle) or not considering their wide musical tastes. Moving between styles does not involve an identity crisis, and may not even be very noticeable; it is seen as reflecting a gradually changing self.

> 'Anne: A bit of a hippy then, wasn't I?... I suppose you could have categorised me in lots of different ways throughout the past, like, six years. Like I started off, like, in the goth-hippy thing, I had, like, long sort of... really long hair that was sort of reddy, sort of normal shades of red, rather than this. And I used to, like, backcomb my hair, but sometimes I didn't, and wore long skirts and lots of black, and so I was more sort of... I was sort of around that. And then I was sort of like hanging around on the goth-rock scene, so I was probably more of a rock-chick thing.
> DM: Did you, when you were like that, did you think of yourself as a...
> Anne: No, it's only looking back that you really notice it.'
> (p121)

Muggleton's respondents did not see their subcultural style as related to a political affiliation, because the emphasis on individuality meant they rejected any affiliation. Subcultural styles did not embody any kind of collective resistance towards a dominant ideology. Resistance was expressed at the individual level in terms of freedom and rejection of constraints. The respondents were also unenthusiastic about fashion and the media.

Muggleton argues that subculturalists define themselves in terms of a series of traits (authentic, individual, open-minded, minority, and so on) which they contrast with the supposed traits of others who are inauthentic. He goes on to argue that while some of these traits can be seen as postmodern, others, such as the emphasis on personal freedom and liberation, have been present in Western culture for two hundred years as aspects of Romanticism. He sees modernity as, since its beginnings, having both a rational mainstream and Romantic countercultures. The subcultural styles of today are as much a continuation of the Romantic countercultures as they are newly postmodern.

IMPORTANCE The question of what has happened to youth subcultures continues to engage sociologists. Muggleton's highly qualitative, detailed study of a small number of individuals who have adopted clearly alternative styles sheds some light on the question. Subcultures today are better referred to as subcultural styles, for subcultures no longer exist, if they ever did, in the fixed way the CCCS implied. There are now styles to which people commit themselves at a deeper level than is implied by the characterisation of postmodern style as 'mix and match', yet not so deeply that they do not continuously move on to develop new styles. The idea that these styles are also distinctively postmodern is also shown to be flawed, for there are continuities with earlier youth styles in the value placed on authenticity and freedom.

EVALUATION

Muggleton selected his respondents by their appearance; the outcome of this was that his sample was in no way representative. His respondents were exceptionally knowledgeable about aspects of youth culture, popular culture and fashion, and many had some involvement in creative or artistic activity (working in record shops, graphic design, as part-time DJs, through studies, and so on). The meaning of style to these individuals cannot be taken as typical of less clearly 'subcultural' individuals or groups, or of young people in general.

His sample was also very small. This had the advantage of allowing in-depth interviews and some detailed probing, but means that any generalisations are dubious. Muggleton selects extracts from interviews to illustrate points about subcultural styles, but does not attempt to quantify the extent to which responses support particular ideas or hypotheses. Although based on such small numbers, the findings are used to develop a theoretical account of the development of styles in relation to Romanticism, postmodernism and class difference. Evidence from a different or wider sample might support alternative interpretations.

QUESTIONS

KNOWLEDGE AND UNDERSTANDING

1. Identify three criticisms that can be made of what Muggleton calls 'the CCCS approach'.
2. What type of interview did Muggleton use? Explain how this differs from other types of interview.
3. What is meant by an 'interview schedule'?
4. What sampling method did Muggleton use?
5. What is meant by 'style-surfing'?
6. How do subculturalists reconcile the conviction that their style is authentic with movement between styles?
7. Why is it more appropriate to refer to subcultural styles rather than subcultures?

ANALYSIS

1. Evaluate the sampling method used by Muggleton. Compare it with one other way in which a sample could have been obtained.
2. Are the subcultural styles of today postmodern according to Muggleton?
3. How might supporters of the CCCS approach counter Muggleton's claims? Evaluate the strengths and weaknesses of both sets of conflicting views.

References Hall, S and Jefferson, T (1976), *Resistance Through Rituals*, Hutchinson, London
Hebdige, D (1979), *Subculture: The Meaning of Style*, Methuen, London
Mungham, G and Pearson, G (1978), *Working-class Youth Culture*, Routledge, London
Widdicombe, S and Wooffitt, R (1995), *The Language of Youth Subcultures: Social Identity in Action*, Harvester Wheatsheaf, Hemel Hempstead
Willis, P (1978), *Profane Culture*, Routledge, London

METAL HEADS:
HEAVY METAL MUSIC AND ADOLESCENT ALIENATION

Jeffrey Jensen Arnett

Westview Press, Boulder, 1996

CONTEXT

This is a study of a particular youth subculture, and of a subculture that (Arnett argues) tells us some important things about youth, community and society today. Arnett is a professor of human development and family studies in the USA, and so it is not surprising that his research and commentary on his findings range beyond a narrow sociological study. Arnett's interest in heavy-metal fans arose from a suggestion by one of his students on who was a 'metal head'. Arnett then went to a Metallica concert, finding it 'fascinating and also disturbing', and decided to research metal heads and their subculture. He says, though, that after attending many concerts and listening to many tapes he has not been converted. He respects how fans feel about this music rather than being able to share in their enjoyment of it!

The few previous academic studies of metal heads and their subculture have also been American. These drew on the British neo-Marxist interpretation of youth subcultures as expressions of working-class resistance to an oppressive capitalist culture. An interpretation of metal heads in this tradition would see the violence and anger in the music and lyrics as a protest against the denial of opportunities to young people by capitalist society. Arnett notes two immediate problems with this: that heavy metal music appeals at least as much to middle-class as to working-class youth, and that the lyrics have very little to do with capitalism or economic issues.

At the outset of any research, it is important to clarify the key terms being used. One problem Arnett faced here was exactly what was meant by 'heavy metal'. Arnett excluded hard rock (for example, Guns n' Roses) because he quickly saw that much of this was qualitatively different from the music that most of his respondents saw as 'real' heavy metal.

The dominant theme in Arnett's commentary on his findings is 'adolescent alienation', a phrase used in the subtitle of the book. Here Arnett agrees with a number of earlier sociologists and other writers who were concerned by what they saw as the decline of family and community values, especially in the USA. His references here include Robert Bellah et al.'s Habits of the Heart (1985) and Amitai Etzioni (1993) on community. He even refers to Durkheim's Suicide (1897), arguing that the lyrics and the lives of metal heads show what Durkheim called anomie and he calls alienation. Arnett also puts these concerns in a wider cross-cultural context by referring to findings by anthropologists about socialisation and the transition from childhood to adulthood in other cultures.

METHODS

Arnett's main method was interviews. He used a list of 31 questions that were designed to get his respondents talking and produced mainly qualitative data. 108 metal heads, 70 boys and 38 girls, were interviewed. The boys were interviewed in Atlanta, Georgia, and the girls in Atlanta and in Cambridge, Massachusetts. They were aged between 13- and 25-years-old. He located the metal heads by putting up a notice in a music store and offering a free cassette of their choice to those who agreed to take part. This was a self-selected sample, and it is not surprising that many respondents were willing to talk at length. Arnett interviewed the male metal-heads himself and female research assistants interviewed the girls. The interview consisted of 31 questions, covering not only heavy metal but also family, religious beliefs, politics and plans, and hopes for the future.

The respondents were also asked to complete several questionnaires. Arnett compared this questionnaire data with data obtained from 118 boys who had been identified as preferring other kinds of music and who were from local high schools or college classes, and from 199 girls who were not heavy-metal fans. This comparison group made it possible for Arnett to see whether, and in what ways, metal heads differed from other young people.

Although his main interest is in what heavy metal means to its fans and its place in their lives, Arnett also felt it important to analyse the music and the words of songs. He carried out a content analysis of lyrics of 115 heavy-metal songs from albums released between 1988 and 1992, all the songs on two albums from each of six selected bands (three mainstream metal bands and three speed/thrash metal bands). In deciding which albums to choose, he excluded hard rock because of the more hedonistic nature of the lyrics. Those albums he chose would, he argues, be recognised by his respondents as being central to heavy metal as they recognised it. Although song lyrics, like all media products, can be interpreted in different ways, Arnett argues that the heavy-metal subculture provides a common way of interpreting the music for his respondents. He analysed songs in three ways.

1 By whether they were written in a major or minor key (minor keys convey negative moods).
2 By the mood of the song, using four categories – anger, sadness/hopelessness, fear and any positive emotions.
3 By lyrical theme (such as drug and alcohol use, Satan, myths and legends).

The findings of the interviews are presented not only within the chapters of the book, but also in the form of short, three- or four-page pen portraits of individual metal heads in between each chapter. These nine profiles (eight boys, one girl) quote extensively from the interviews and also contain a summary of factual information, including such items as number of heavy-metal recordings owned, goals in ten years, and illegal or anti-social behaviour over the past year.

KEY FINDINGS

In some respects metal heads are quite different from other young people.

Metal heads engage in more reckless behaviour than other boys; for example, they are more likely to drive while drunk or have sex without contraception. There is therefore a correlation between being a metal head and engaging in reckless behaviour. Arnett argues, however, that one does not cause the other; rather, both result from seeking new exciting experiences.

In fact, many metal heads say that the music calms them down or allows them to release anger in a non-violent way. Arnett discusses the practice at gigs of 'slamdancing' in which aggression is released in a way that causes remarkably little harm.

Metal heads are more likely than other boys to see their parents as near-equals rather than as having authority over them. This suggests their parents have practised a style of socialisation that emphasises freedom of choice and tolerance. Arnett argues that young people are often given adult freedoms without being required to contribute to the household. Metal heads are more likely to have divorced parents and Arnett suggests there are also correlations with the breakdown of extended family ties (for example, rarely seeing grandparents) and with frequently moving house so there is no sense of involvement in a community. Arnett sees these as general trends within American society, not as specific to the families of metal heads.

Metal heads often see their futures in terms of music or related activities, such as playing in a heavy-metal band or writing for a music magazine.

Arnett interprets the appeal of heavy metal as fulfilling a need for excitement and sensation-seeking among young men. American patterns of upbringing strongly emphasise individuality and independence. Arnett contends that, in the absence of strong family and community ties, this can lead to a sense of alienation. 'By alienation I mean a sense of estrangement from one's own culture, a deep loneliness arising from a lack of gratifying emotional connections to others, and cynicism about the ideas and possibilities for life offered by one's culture' (p17). Other cultures provide rituals to mark the transition to manhood, often channelling a need for sensation. American society fails to do this, and heavy-metal subculture is one response to this failure.

Findings of the content analysis:

- 96 of 115 sings were in a minor key
- 50% of songs could be categorised as based on anger, 31% on sadness, 10% on fear and 15% on positive feelings
- the most common themes were violence (40 songs), angst (35) and protest (21). Some themes which might have been expected but which were rarely present were alcohol and substance abuse.

Overall, Arnett finds that the content analysis supports his contention about heavy metal music as an expression of alienation.

IMPORTANCE This is not just a book about a fascinating and highly visible youth subculture. Arnett uses the example of metal heads to investigate the nature of socialisation in American society, both within families and within agencies of socialisation such as religious institutions and schools. He addresses many concerns that have been expressed by a wide range of commentators. His attitude to metal heads is open and positive where appropriate; it is the changes in society that have produced the metal-head subculture that he condemns. He goes beyond the strictly sociological, or social scientific, and gives a powerful message to parents and others: there is no point condemning the loudness and the apparent violence of the music, and the way to counter heavy metal's appeal to millions of young Americans is to provide socialisation that values mutual obligation, responsibility and interdependence.

EVALUATION

Arnett's research gives us a full and interesting account of a particular subculture. He uses his findings, however, to build an analysis of American society and in particular of socialisation, which is contentious. Arnett's main interest in his findings is in the ways in which they support his argument about the difficult transition to manhood for boys in American society today. Thus he focuses strongly on the alienation he says metal heads experience, seeing metal heads as one particularly visible manifestation of a deep set of problems affecting many young people. At this level his argument can be questioned. The qualitative data presented in the book (for example, in the profiles and quotations from interviews) have been selected from a much larger body of material and may have been selected to support Arnett's case. In particular, Arnett's narrow definition of heavy-metal music (which he fully discusses) excludes music others might have included (for example, hard-rock bands such as Poison and Guns N' Roses) and that would have changed the picture he draws of heavy metal.

Like most studies of subcultures, this research is limited in time and space. Most of Arnett's respondents were from one city (although many had lived elsewhere) and his sample cannot be claimed to be representative. However, Arnett uses his findings to justify much wider criticism of American society as characterised by 'hyper-individualism'.

One of the problems studies of youth subcultures have always faced is that boys almost always dominate subcultures. Arnett has only one chapter on girls, and there is one profile of a female metal-head. He argues, however, that this is justified, first because the heavy-metal subculture is largely male and, second, because the case of girls fits far less easily into his argument about the difficulties of the transition to adulthood. There *are* girl metal heads, and it would be a worthwhile research project in itself to investigate the attractions of the heavy-metal subculture for girls.

By Arnett's own interpretation, the appeal of heavy metal is likely to be different and less strong in Britain, where hyper-individualism has not become so pronounced. Again, a research project could investigate what heavy metal means to its followers here.

QUESTIONS

KNOWLEDGE AND UNDERSTANDING

1 What kind of interviews did this research use?
2 What is meant by a 'self-selected sample'?
3 What does Arnett mean by alienation? (Do not copy the quotation; try to express the idea in your own way.)
4 In what three ways did Arnett analyse the content of heavy-metal music?
5 What did he find was the most common theme of the lyrics?
6 What does Arnett mean by 'hyper-individualism'?

ANALYSIS

1 Why do you think the girls in this research were interviewed by female interviewers?
2 How significant is it that Arnett does not particularly like heavy metal? Would better research be produced by a metal head?
3 Why does heavy metal appeal less to girls than to boys?
4 To what extent do you think similar conclusions could be drawn about other music-based subcultures that you know of?

References Bellah, R N, Madsen, R, Sullivan, W M, Swidler, A and Tipton, S M (1985), *Habits of the Heart: Individualism and Commitment in American Life*, Harper and Row, New York
Durkheim, E (1979), *Suicide: A Study in Sociology*, Routledge, London (originally 1897)
Etzioni, A (1993), *The Spirit of Community: Rights, Responsibilities and the Communitarian Agenda*, Crown, New York

THE FAMILY AND COMMUNITY LIFE OF OLDER PEOPLE

Chris Phillipson, Miriam Bernard, Judith Phillips and Jim Ogg

Routledge, London, 2001

CONTEXT

This research, funded by the Economic and Social Research Council as part of their research programme on Population and Household Change, revisited three areas that had been the subject of classic studies of family and community life in the 1940s and 1950s. These were Bethnal Green in the East End of London (*Family and Kinship in East London* by Michael Young and Peter Willmott, 1957, and *The Family Life of Old People* by Peter Townsend, 1957), Woodford, a suburban area in Essex (*Family and Class in a London Suburb* by Young and Willmott, 1960) and Wolverhampton in the Midlands (*The Social Medicine of Old Age* by Sheldon, 1948). Young and Willmott's two books were not specifically about the experiences of older people, but investigated these as one aspect of family and community life. Young and Willmott's Woodford book studied changes in family and community life when families who had previously lived in the East End of London were relocated to new suburban developments.

The aim of the research was to research the family and community life of older people in these three areas and, by comparing the findings with those of the earlier baseline studies, to discover what changes and developments had taken place. The period during which the baseline studies were conducted was characterised by a widespread belief in better times to come (improvements in health and education, more consumer goods, and so on) alongside the survival of, for example, slum housing and rationing. Many older people in the baseline studies had grown up in poverty, and in old age found themselves without clear social roles (especially men). During the 1950s the new social category of 'teenager' – young people with spending power – emerged. In rapidly changing times older people clung, when they could, to the security provided by the extended family.

By the 1990s, the social context of old age had changed significantly. There were greater conflicts and divisions within society and the nuclear family was fragmenting. Inequalities had widened and there was a widespread perception of inner-city areas as beset by poverty and crime. Old age itself had also changed, with greater opportunities for some to take on new roles – the 'third age' of activity and leisure – but for many difficult choices (such as how and to what extent to maintain contact with relatives and friends after one of their children had divorced).

METHODS

The research involved two phases. The first phase consisted of questionnaires returned by 627 older people from the three areas selected for the research. The researchers used a random sample drawn from the registers of General Practitioners in these areas. The baseline studies had involved 203 people in Bethnal Green, 210 older people in Woodford and Wanstead and 477 in Wolverhampton. Phillipson *et al.* aimed for about 200 respondents in each area, and obtained 195 in Bethnal Green, 204 in Woodford and 228 in Wolverhampton. The response rates were respectively 63%, 65% and 78%.

The baseline studies had taken retirement age (65 for men, 60 for women) as the criterion for selection, and so also did Phillipson *et al.*'s research. The samples were stratified by age and gender, and also by ethnicity in the case of Bethnal Green. 62% of respondents were women and 38% men, reflecting the proportions of older men and women in the population. Bethnal Green had, in fact, slightly more men than women in the final sample because there were very few older Bangladeshi women and so almost all Bangladeshis sampled were men. The sample's marital status closely reflected that predicted by other research: 55% married, 31% widowed, 9% single, 5% divorced or separated.

The second phase involved in-depth interviews producing qualitative data. These were the source of the many quotations used throughout the book to illustrate points. Interviews were conducted with 62 people aged over 75 who had indicated in the first phase that they were willing to take part. There were also 18 interviews with younger people who were named by these respondents as being part of their social network. Finally, there were 23 interviews with Bangladeshi and Punjabi families in Bethnal Green and Wolverhampton, and two group interviews with people working with older members of these ethnic groups.

The questions in the questionnaire and interview were designed to investigate seven main issues.

1 Changes in household composition
2 Changes in the geographical proximity of kin and relatives
3 Extent and type of help provided by family
4 Contact and relationship with neighbours
5 Relationships with friends
6 Involvement in social and leisure activities
7 Experiences of minority ethnic-groups.

KEY FINDINGS

The main finding of the research is that over the past 50 years there has been a shift from old age being experienced within the family group to old age being shaped within personal communities in which friends may be as important as immediate family.

In terms of household composition more older people live alone, or just with a partner, and fewer live in households containing more than one generation. Children and other relatives often lived nearby, but were more dispersed, and many older people named friends and neighbours among those they were closest to. Growing old is experienced more often now as part of a couple. Even where children live nearby, those children will have other commitments and the relationship with parents has to be accommodated with these. The support that is provided now has to be negotiated. Moreover, children of elderly parents are now themselves often experiencing retirement or health problems of late middle-age.

The experience of growing old in the community – shown in, for example, interaction with neighbours – varied considerably between the different areas. Bethnal Green seemed to have lost the strong sense of community it had had in the 1950s, so that some people were afraid to go out, especially at night. In Woodford, on the other hand, older people had more relatives and friends and this reduced such fears.

In his study, Townsend had seen retirement for men as involving loss of status and creating difficulties in finding things to do. The home was seen as female territory and men were expected to be out in the day, even if they had nowhere to go. Phillipson *et al.* found a different attitude to retirement: about half of all respondents saw it as 'a new phase in your life'. A minority did, however, see retirement as having negative aspects.

Leisure in old age had changed substantially since the 1950s. The main leisure activity today is reading whereas older people fifty years ago would have given up reading when they left school at an early age. Television has become important for many older people. Gardening and looking after the house are also important today. These, along with television and reading, show how leisure has become centred on the home and how it is experienced alone or as part of a couple. People are active in old age but the activity is often in a particular and narrow social world.

The two minority ethnic groups studied, Bangladeshi and Punjabi, were similar in that older people were surrounded by family, either living with them or close by. Women's roles were focused very much on providing care while for older men religion was an important part of daily life. Respondents had strong emotional ties to family members in Bangladesh or India, although returning there in old age was not seen as possible. There were also some differences between the two groups. Overall, the researchers felt that the presence of family support often concealed problems of isolation and deprivation, and a sense of having left one home without being fully accepted in the new home.

IMPORTANCE This research provides an excellent example of the use of baseline studies to compare changes over time. This places a limit on the research – comparisons can only be made with data gathered in the baseline studies. The studies chosen, however, provided sufficient material on the lives of the older people to enable statements to be made about changes over time. The research provides evidence of changes in the experience of old age related to changes both in wider society and in local communities. It provides insights into how much life has changed over 50 years in the areas studied. Old age has become a time of greater opportunities yet of greater uncertainties.

EVALUATION

Throughout the book the researchers try at the same time to give generalisations and to show the distinctiveness of change and life in each of the three areas. In a sense, these are three research projects in one (or four, if one counts the consideration of older people from minority ethnic groups separately). It is important to bear in mind that the generalisations are based on only three areas, and that the experiences of older people there are not necessarily typical of the English working class, yet alone older people in Britain as a whole.

The use of the baseline studies for comparison makes it possible to highlight important changes in the lives of older people in the three areas. Again, it is important to bear in mind that each area has had a different history over the intervening 50 years. It is difficult to be sure to what extent the often bleak descriptions of the lives of the older people in, particularly, Bethnal Green arise from a specific set of circumstances that have eroded community spirit there.

The topic of family relationships and support is a difficult one to investigate. The use by the researchers of personal network diagrams provides a part solution to this, allowing respondents to show degrees of closeness and support from both family and friends. There remains the problem that some of the key words used in gathering data, such as 'close' and 'important' are difficult to define exactly and may be interpreted differently by different respondents.

QUESTIONS

KNOWLEDGE AND UNDERSTANDING

1. What is meant by 'baseline studies'?
2. Which two studies by Young and Willmott were among the baseline studies used for this research?
3. What sampling frame was used?
4. By which three social characteristics was the sample stratified?
5. Why were more men than women interviewed in Bethnal Green?
6. What was the key finding of the research?
7. What is the main leisure activity of older people today?

ANALYSIS

1. Choose any three sociological research studies you are familiar with and evaluate their usefulness as baseline studies for future research.
2. In what ways do men and women experience the transition to old age differently?
3. What can the changes described here tell us about changes in family life more generally?

References Sheldon, J H (1948), *The Social Medicine of Old Age*, Oxford University Press, Oxford
Townsend, P (1957), *The Family Life of Old People*, Penguin, Harmondsworth
Willmott, P and Young, M (1960), *Family and Class in a London Suburb*, Routledge, London
Young, M and Willmott, P (1961), *Family and Kinship in East London*, Penguin, Harmondsworth

UNCERTAIN MASCULINITIES:
YOUTH, ETHNICITY AND CLASS IN CONTEMPORARY BRITAIN

Mike O Donnell and Sue Sharpe

Routledge, London, 2000

CONTEXT

There is an increasingly strong trend both in society and in sociology to see boys and men as a problem. The evidence to support this view is strong: they do less well in school, they commit more crime and their suicide rates are high in comparison with females of the same age. Furthermore, the under-performance of males in a whole range of social areas makes many of them poor-value as life partners for women and economically problematic for society as they progress from failure to failure.

Whilst a large amount has been written about male friendships and male youth culture, much of this work is very dated or is framed within a social context in which males are seen as the dominant and more interesting gender. Furthermore, there is an intense social debate in which masculinity has been claimed to be in crisis due to the challenges issued by the feminist movement and the rise in the social status of women. This type of view is typical of masculinist and right-wing thinking but also has a following among left-wing writers such as Bea Campbell (1993) – who claims that the loss of males from the family has led to an over-aggressive notion of masculinity in young men based on media icons such as Arnold Schwarznegger in the *Terminator* films.

O'Donnell and Sharpe are therefore exploring masculinity as it is in the context of a process of change and redefinition. They are concerned with the way that young men on the verge of adulthood construct their notions of what it is to be a man in modern society. They further acknowledge that there are a variety of notions of masculinity available to young men that relate to ethnicity and social class. They see that some themes of masculinity are cross-cultural (such as an overwhelming interest in sport and popular culture) but that ethnicity plays a part in shaping male identities.

The aims of the study were to:

- look at key areas of male lives to discover how boys develop an identity that they can conceive of as masculine
- investigate the extent to which men find discovering their own male identities problematical and difficult
- explore the widespread perception that boys are problems for society.

METHODS

The research was conducted in the mid-1990s. Questionnaires were completed by 262 boys in four London schools. The boys were aged between 15 and 16 and were generally in Year 11. Three of the schools were in Ealing and were the same schools that Sue Sharpe had used as the basis of her 1994 study into femininity. A fourth school from Hackney, a deprived London borough, was added to the sample. The largest ethnic groups in the study were white, African-Caribbean and Asians, including Sikhs and Moslems. There were a variety of boys from different social classes, but some patterns did emerge: African boys tended to be middle class whereas African-Caribbean boys were more likely to be from working-class homes.

From this initial sample, a further 44 boys were interviewed. Three senior teaching staff were also interviewed. Interviewing techniques would appear to have been largely flexible. In most of the material quoted the interviewer seems to be clarifying the responses of the boys to the line of questioning by simply repeating or rephrasing the previous final statement that the boys had made. This study did not make use of classroom observation and rejected this methodology. The authors suggested that classroom observation studies often lead to accusations of negative labelling of students by teachers, and that few boys actually felt that they were unfairly treated. They also claimed that teachers who do label would, in reality, find themselves disciplined.

KEY FINDINGS

There are five chapters discussing findings, each of which explores an element of masculinity and the lives of the boys who participated in the study.

GENDER AND RACE EQUALITY

Schools were discovered to have strong and visible policies about gender equality, however, despite the equalising effect of the National Curriculum, some gendering of subject choices still occurs. This was particularly significant in the case of sport where football is not just a game but a key part of the creation of a male identity and male culture. Many of the boys were sympathetic to school attempts to support gender equality and race equality in their questionnaires.

Boys seemed to see teachers as 'advocates and enforcers of anti-racism' (p29). Although the researchers were unwilling to discount racism on the part of teachers, racism was more likely to be a feature of peer groups than a feature of the schools studied. Often this racism took the form of unpleasant joking. Racism was not necessarily white on black either; Indian and Pakistani boys engaged in racist behaviour towards each other, with Sikhs and Hindus engaged in conflicts with Moslems. Serious racism occurred outside school and boys would feel vulnerable in neighbourhoods that were not their own.

Some boys were harming themselves through being troublesome and difficult both in school and out of it. However, masculine posturing and macho behaviours were less likely to be aimed at women than at other boys. Many of the boys made statements supporting equality and condemning racism but their daily behaviours showed that what they said and what they did could be different. This is a significant finding of the study – the way that boys were able to hold contradictory attitudes – and is reflected in the word 'uncertain' in the title.

THE SOCIAL CONSTRUCTION OF YOUTHFUL MASCULINITIES

This chapter tends to focus on peer groups and ethnicity in the formation of notions of masculinity. However, the authors note that there are a variety of other factors that influence men in their creation of social identities: class, location and the ethos of the school itself. Sharpe and O'Donnell are at pains to point out that schools operate according to stated anti-racist and anti-sexist policies, and that boys often express these views in school but use a different set of moral values at home and at leisure.

Interestingly, the authors did not discover the strongly developed, class-based anti-school cultures such as those described by Willis (1977) and Hargreaves (1967). The boys usually referred to individual trouble-makers and to one small group that was self styled as the 'underachievers'. Masculinity among boys was still notable because of the desire of boys to dominate social situations. Many boys were confused because they had learned something from the equality agenda but also retained significantly sexist and racist attitudes. The authors claim that these views derive from the home and the media more than they do from the schools, but this remains an unanswered question because the home attitudes were not studied.

MARRIAGE, FAMILY AND RELATIONSHIPS

This is an important chapter in the light of moral panics about the status of marriage in our society. Some interesting social shifts are noted, with boys expecting traditional marriages and having positive views of what marriage will mean for them, and girls being far more cautious in their views about married relationships and less willing than men to consider that they will marry. This leads to male insecurities. Increasingly, there is a less consistent view of what it is to be a man in our society, so men are required to be macho as well as sensitive and caring. This is an uneasy path to tread for a boy, because there are 'contradictions stemming from the continuing power and the increasing fragility of masculinity'. This, the authors feel, accounted for the existence of a clear distinction between the views that the boys expressed and their actual behaviour. Boys who did not express the appropriately masculine norms of the groups were the victims of bullying and homophobia. There was an implicit assumption that sporting types could not be homosexual and that quiet and intelligent boys were prone to homosexuality. Rejection of homosexuality was particularly notable among African and Asian boys.

WORK

One of the most significant changes in the structure of British society has been to the type and nature of work. Women are more significant in the workplace and unskilled labour is not needed, so unemployment is high among the unqualified. Boys cannot leave school and be assured of jobs as they once were. They still tend to aim for work that is traditionally seen as male work, but this may be logical since male employment is generally higher paid than female work. There has been a shift from manual labour as the main aspiration of boys, to high-tech occupations such as design or computing. Significantly higher numbers of Asian males chose futures in business and finance. Middle-class boys had higher career aspirations. Boys felt that life is harder for them in terms of employment than it was for their fathers. There are still significant differences in terms of aspiration and employment for boys because of existing social inequalities of class, ethnicity, and gender.

CULTURE, LEISURE AND CRIME

Boys seemed to wish to avoid the world of adults and there is a significant market of clothes and items aimed at the youth market. Masculinity and conceptions of masculinity drive much of the culture of young males and this youth culture feeds on crude images and depictions of aggression, racism and sexism. The edge of much of this material is softened by its presentation as humour. Some boys realised that girls were dismayed by masculine dominant behaviour and interested in sensitivity but this recognition was not enough to put them off crude displays of 'macho'. Boys are attracted to and desire girls, but still need to define themselves as 'not feminine' by rejecting the social changes that females require of them. Men are not adjusting to changes in gender patterns as quickly as women, and their reactions are defensive. Although those reactions are marked by ethnic and class differences, 'laddishness' is a feature of these responses. This, however, is a more gentle and mocking naughtiness than the aggressive posturing of some earlier youth sub-cultures such as the skinheads and punks.

IMPORTANCE

This study has a large sample-frame which makes it reliable and it clearly has a great deal of validity in terms of representing the culture of young men because their words are used so often as supporting evidence. The picture of masculinity offered is one that is more commonplace and recognisable than that normally provided by the intense ethnographic studies of small groups of the disaffected. We have a pen portrait of a generation of men who are adjusting to a world where their traditional rights as males are being challenged, but at the same time where the pace of change is not as fast as some commentators would have us believe.

EVALUATION

This study has a far wider brief than many ethnographic studies. There is less exciting reference to episodes or relationships that the researcher experienced during the research process than in some similar studies, and this gives the material a cooler and more measured feel. The size of the sample offers the opportunity to discuss trends and patterns discovered in the data, but because interviews were used, the voices of the boys can be heard in the discussions.

The authors note that although the boys are slow to respond to some of the social changes occurring as a result of changes in the role of women, the picture is one that is generally positive. It is clear that the authors liked and responded to their subjects but with a degree of emotional detachment that enabled them to present a positive picture of young men. They are able to distance themselves by calling their subjects 'boys' and 'young people'. This language is significant because the sociologists are clearly studying a group of which they are not a part.

The terms of reference are wide ranging and although we are not told how long the questionnaires and interviews took to conduct, they must have been very detailed to elicit the information that was eventually gathered. The findings are not easy to summarise, simply because of their complexity and breadth.

This study is considerably more sympathetic to the aims of schools and of teachers than much sociology over the past twenty years or so. There is a genuine sense that all parties were of interest to the research team and that the voices of those who have some influence over the young were of value to the team. Although not within the scope of the study, it would have been interesting to hear from parents of young men to consider to what extent the views they expressed are generated from their peer groups rather than their homes.

QUESTIONS

KNOWLEDGE AND UNDERSTANDING

1 Why was it considered necessary to study boys and young men?
2 What were the aims of this research?
3 How large was the sample frame used by the researchers?
4 Suggest reasons why the researchers chose to focus on boys in their final year of compulsory schooling.
5 To what extent do schools encourage racism and sexism among young men?
6 Suggest reasons why boys are less reluctant than boys to consider conventional married relationships.
7 Suggest reasons why such large-scale projects are so difficult for the individual researcher to carry out.

ANALYSIS

1 What practical problems did the researchers face in conducting this study?
2 Are studies of one gender alone justified in the light of our present sociological understandings of the nature of sexism?
3 To what extent can the findings of Sharpe and O'Donnell be considered to be relevant to studies of gender patterns in the early 2000s?
4 Evaluate the work of Sharpe and O'Donnell under each of the following headings: practicality, reliability, ethics, validity, and representativeness.

References Campbell, B (1993), *Goliath*, Lime Tree, London
Hargreaves, D (1967), *Social Relations in a Secondary School*, Routledge, London
Sharpe, S (1994) *Just Like a Girl*, (second edition), Penguin, Harmondsworth
Willis P (1977), *Learning to Labour*, Ashgate, Aldershot

THE COMPANY SHE KEEPS:
AN ETHNOGRAPHY OF GIRLS' FRIENDSHIPS

Valerie Hey

Open University Press, Buckingham, 1997

CONTEXT

This study was written within the context of feminist sociology and concerns an ethnographic study of girls and their friendships in two London comprehensive schools. The fieldwork was conducted in the 1980s.

There has been a large amount written on male subcultures, youth cultures and friendship groupings in the sociologies of education, deviance and culture. Many of these studies ignore young females, seeing them as merely bit-part players in the dramatic accounts of male relationships. The male subjects of many ethnographic studies are dismissive of females, seeing them as domestic creatures or as sexual prey. While this may be understandable, what is also significant is that the researchers themselves ignore the domestic lives of their subjects and their interactions with women, despite the fact that many come from female-dominated households. Young girls are seen as conformists and, therefore, as uninteresting compared with the exciting, dangerous and rebellious males. Even the best of these studies tend to do no more than merely acknowledge females, rather than paying attention to female perceptions of the social world.

Friendship, too, is a very under-researched phenomenon. We know it exists and that it has different rules for males and for females, but there has been very little attempt to identify the nature and dynamics of friendships – despite the very well-known fact that many adolescent females have intense emotional relationships in which 'best friends' and groups of same-sex friends are very significant. Valerie Hey's work is an attempt to redress the balance by providing a first-hand account of female emotional dynamics. In doing this she is also rejecting the masculine nature of the existing theories that account for youth culture – theories that, she claims, are really accounts of male cultures.

The aims of the study were to:

- investigate how girls create their identities through talking and writing
- gain an understanding of the processes that take place in girls' social networks
- recognise how females negotiate their relationships with an outside world that is male-dominated
- investigate the way that girls create intensely pleasurable, emotional 'lived' personal lives in the face of gendered repression.

METHODS

Valerie Hey provides a very detailed account of her work, but, because this text is ethnographic, many of the techniques emerge through her accounts of her findings. Certainly, she had a difficult time while conducting this work and some of her techniques were developed while the work progressed as a result of a significant incident or a sudden insight. This does not mean that it was unplanned – on the contrary, it was highly organised – but Hey herself was also flexible enough to see where the plan required adaptation to situations as they emerged. She reveals elements of her biography and emotional states in her discussion of female friendships. She also refers to some of the issues that arose from being a female researcher conducting a study in a school in which gender equality was sensitive and challenging to both the hierarchy of the school and the staff themselves.

The initial study school was 'Eastford' School, which was a large mixed comprehensive. The second was 'Crossfield', a smaller single-sex school in a working-class area. Eastford School was experiencing difficulty during the course of the study. Hey implies that there was weak management and low morale in a divided and hostile institution. She experienced some ridicule and harassment from male pupils and staff which she interprets as a response to her interest in females being seen as in some way threatening by the males. Her move to Crossfield was negotiated by the Head of Eastford. Here she was more successful and, since it was a female institution, she was helped by the support networks that women establish among themselves.

Hey offers a detailed account of the procedures and sources of information that she used. These were varied and imaginative. She is open about her own inexperience and relates stories about situations where her misunderstandings exposed her to ridicule or embarrassment. She was also in the awkward position of being older than the girls. Although she is an ex-teacher, she was still a stranger attempting to penetrate an intimate and private set of relationships with an emotionally fraught, negotiated and largely unexplored set of rules.

- Hey spent her time with girls doing what they were doing: attending lessons, going on cross-country runs and even truanting! The girls tested Hey to see whether she would tell their teachers of their misbehaviour.
- Hey is open about the fact that there was a trading situation occurring. She would exchange small gifts of time, sometimes money, excuses to miss lessons, attention and advice in return for access to information about the girls' social lives and emotions. Hey, as a result of her experience, suggests that ethnographic research requires considerable ethical compromise that is often denied or avoided in subsequent accounts by researchers.
- Hey made friends with girls, and sometimes these relationships were fairly close so that the girls were able to explain the meanings of their slang and the social context in which exchanges were occurring. One particular study group of working-class girls (led by Jude) were frequent truants and so Hey necessarily spent time with them outside school. Some of these friendships were with individuals and these form some of the case studies.
- One of her main sources of data was provided by the notes that girls wrote to each other in class. She collected a wide variety of these and was also given examples by sympathetic staff. Girls gave her examples of notes that had been saved for long periods of time, years in some cases.

KEY FINDINGS

Girls often need to keep their friendships with each other invisible. Teachers may frown upon emotional behaviour among the girls that they teach; frequently these friendships only emerge into the public domain when they create discipline problems for the school. Girls use strategies to keep their emotional discussions and negotiations private and this includes the practice of note-writing. (Interestingly, mobile telephones were not common at the time that this research was conducted, but this need for privacy and seclusion may account for the great popularity nowadays of text-messaging and instant messaging among the young.)

Cliques tend to form among girls of the same social class. They involve a core of best friends and others who move in and out of favour with the core groups. There is much jostling and negotiating within these groups, with some girls acting in competition with each other for the company of a favoured partner. Middle-class girls have more freedom and autonomy in terms of sexual behaviours but are often seen as 'boffins' and unattractive sexually by the working-class girls. Conversely, working-class girls are dangerous and excluding to middle-class girls who reject what they see as the over-feminised and over-sexualised behaviour of the working-class girls.

Girls may strive to dominate a clique, and in one study group Hey observed a strategic campaign by one girl who was relatively affluent and therefore able to offer invitations and gifts. This was resisted by the group who saw her quest for popularity and domination as a search for power. Eventually she was socially excluded by the group and changed schools. The characteristics of friendship required by a girl are: reliability, reciprocity, commitment, confidentiality, trust and sharing.

Girls are constantly engaged in complex judgemental processes and part of the power of a group is represented by the ability to exclude individuals from intimacy. Girls may mis-read their emotional connections, so that one would describe another as 'best friend' whereas in response the relationship is seen as 'casual'. This is socially dangerous for the girls because each view of the relationship involves a sequence of rules and negotiations. Curiously, the imagery of the insults used to exclude a girl is based upon her relative physical attractiveness and her perceived morality. Samples include 'flat-chested' and 'slapper'.

Working-class girls resist schooling through a variety of methods because they associate schooling with snobbery and lack of friends. Non-attendance is one form of rebellion, and the notes themselves are a form of subversion. There is often explicit sexual content in the notes; sometimes to explore and reject the potential for lesbianism in the relationships they form and at other times to insult or distance themselves from another girl or a teacher. They therefore define what is an appropriate model of femininity – one that involves being attractive to boys without in fact having to do 'it'. Heterosexuality can be used by girls, particularly working-class girls who are socially powerless, to manipulate the powerful in their environment; they use their bodies to attract and control men. They have little viable alternative. Hey suggests that until we understand how girls create their notions of femininity for each other and we address issues involving the lived social relationships of women, discourses about equality are unlikely to be fully effective.

IMPORTANCE

This study is of tremendous significance because it attempts to restore the balance of the study of sociology by looking at the social and emotional elements of the lives of females. It uses feminist research techniques to issue a ferocious challenge to previous studies in which women were relegated to being social props in the face of the exciting and extreme behaviour of the males.

EVALUATION

Hey experienced some difficulty in penetrating her target groups initially and worked in the closest detail with girls of a younger age than she originally intended to work with. This meant that she was unable to penetrate Asian and Black friendship groups fully. However, much important discussion does consider the way in which non-white girls were excluded from a high-status clique. Hey acknowledges the implicit racism of the working-class groupings, which she suggests was tacitly supported by the school if not by individual teachers.

As an ethnographer, Hey explains that her relationships with the study groups were fluid and that some girls did drop out of the study. She found it necessary to engage in discussion with the girls, some of whom she found difficult to identify with despite having her own experience of intense emotional friendship, being a mother of daughters and also originating from a working-class home herself. Hey was interested in the development of friendship groupings and so there is little consideration of the more isolated individuals. The implication from the book may seem to be that all girls participate in these relationships, but it is possible that some girls may invest these friendships with more significance than others.

The question of the occurrence of development of these intense friendships between single-sex and gendered schools is not fully developed. Given the course of the fieldwork, it is difficult to see how this could have been attempted but it leaves an unanswered question: does the presence of boys increase or decrease the intensity of female single-sex friendship groups?

Although Hey criticises male sociologists for not looking at the relationship between the home and male subcultures, there is a distinct absence of adults in this book. Although there are accounts of parents interfering in their daughter's relationships and vetoing friends for a variety of reasons, this is not explored as an element of the social dynamics of friendship. Also, many teenage girls and women have intense emotional relationships with their own mothers and it would be interesting to further explore whether these female relationships echo the female friendships that Hey describes.

Hey is far more self-critical of her motivations and personal impact on the research than is common in ethnographic work. A more general pattern for such texts is one in which the researcher states a position that, it is claimed, may influence the results. The statement, once safely and ethically made, is never referred to again by the writer. Hey, however, discusses the editing process in this light and talks of the way in which a respondent may also edit the stories told.

There is little mention of bullying and the bullying nature of girl relationships. There is an activity that is referred to as 'bitching' – a term that rather defuses the actual significance of the activity. 'Bitching' consists of insulting girls who are not part of the group when they are not present to hear what is being said. Hey does not discuss the impact of such behaviour on the least secure members of the social group who are likely themselves to become victims on future occasions. It is possible that in accentuating the positive side to female relationships, Hey is underplaying the sheer frightening nastiness that some of the note-writing and activities imply.

QUESTIONS

KNOWLEDGE AND UNDERSTANDING

1 Why did Hey choose to focus on the friendships of girls?
2 What were the aims of this research?
3 What difficulties did Hey experience in her first study school?
4 What form of content analysis did Hey use? Why was it particularly appropriate to this study?
5 Why do girls find it necessary to keep their friendships secret?
6 How do working-class and middle-class girls differ in their social arrangements and attitudes to each other?
7 Suggest reasons why such small-scale projects are so difficult for the individual researcher to carry out.

ANALYSIS

1 What ethical problems did Hey face in conducting this study?
2 To what extent can the findings of Hey be considered to be an accurate portrait of girls in schools in other areas or from other cultures in the rest of the UK?
3 To what extent can it be claimed that the study of sociology is in fact the study of males? Refer to the work of Hey and other feminists in your answer.

FORMATIONS OF CLASS AND GENDER:
BECOMING RESPECTABLE

Beverley Skeggs

Sage Publications, London, 1997

CONTEXT

This study was written within the context of feminist sociology and concerns an ethnographic study of working-class women. It is also an intensely personal book because Skeggs made friendships within her study group. Many of the issues raised were felt personally by her because she draws on her own aspirant-working-class background to understand the issues facing her study group.

Marxism no longer holds the dominant theoretical position it did in the sociology produced in Britain in the 1960s and 1970s. The growth of the New Right in politics and the failure of Marxism to answer so many theoretical questions have led a lot of commentators away from classic Marxist accounts of society. Postmodernism has gained popularity as a theoretical framework for study and this tends to underplay issues such as class and gender. Skeggs makes a strong case for the return of the analysis of class into debates about gender with this study. This is not, however, a classic Marxist account because it draws on a huge range of references, including postmodern understandings.

The book is primarily concerned with tackling issues of theory. Much of the analysis is concerned with Skeggs' own development into certain awarenesses and forms of thinking. This makes it quite difficult reading; and the book is therefore intended for an adult and academic market – despite its subject matter being concerned with life as lived by ordinary women.

METHODS

There is very little direct description of the methods used. This is a form of ethnography that draws on the feminist view that all understandings are relative. Information about the sampling is minimal. Skeggs points out that although she was researching her group for some time, the aim of her study changed as her own interests and concerns developed.

Her research was longitudinal and lasted for 12 years, including three years of full-time participant observation. The sample consisted of 83 white women from the north-west of England (Lancashire). It began when many of the women enrolled on a Caring course at a college and follows them through their subsequent lives. The focus is on how the women create a sense of self, and the part that social class and the search for respectability plays in female working-class identity. Skeggs supports her observations with biographies of the women, information about the local and national economy, and interviews with the women, their partners, friends and teachers. She also lived in the community of the women she studied, with whom she shared many life experiences (being herself a school leaver at 16 and a late returner to full-time education).

There is limited information offered on the sample, but a reading of the text offers the following.

- 28% experienced disadvantage in the form of abusive fathering, broken homes and disrupted family life.
- They were young, unqualified and concerned with pleasure and going out at the onset of the study but were under pressure to marry and settle as the study progressed.
- The women were enrolled on Caring courses at local colleges.
- Many of the women subsequently entered caring occupations, but not at levels that required training and qualifications.
- 21% of their mothers were full-time housewives and 22% of fathers were self-employed.
- 5% of fathers had disappeared.

Skeggs produced classic feminist research in that she discussed her findings with the study groups and asked for their views of her interpretations.

KEY FINDINGS

Skeggs suggests that low class-position often means exclusion and it is defined by what one does *not have* rather than what one has access to. Many of the women rejected a specifically working-class identity and aspired to respectability. This is an important phrase in the study and refers to a working-class desire to be respected. It is more than that, however. Those who have respectability are not concerned about it, or its existence. Working-class people, however, are seen as dangerous and threatening, and so respectability becomes desirable for them because they wish to see themselves as being as good and as valued as those who do have respectability. Many of the findings of this study illustrate ways in which the working-class women of the study attempt to create and define respectability for themselves.

Many of the women had left school with few qualifications and viewed themselves as educational failures. In addition, the time when the study was conducted was one of exceptionally high unemployment, although northern women have a tradition of working and employment in factories and domestic work. The women had enrolled on Caring courses as a way of training in something they already had experience of, and at which they felt they had a chance of success. They were not negative towards school – indeed, they had enjoyed it as a social experience if not an educational one. The Caring courses, however, had low status and were feminised. Nonetheless, the girls gained a dignity in their Caring courses because they rejected academic subjects as being impractical; here they studied something they knew and fully understood as women. Their identity as carers and their work placements in homes, hospitals and nurseries gave them dignity through the respectability of having a purpose and through a sense of being valued by the people they served. The courses, however, required the girls to evaluate their own family life and practice in a way that was critical of their prior knowledge.

The courses encouraged the girls into a self-identity as a caring person and this involved an enormous amount of selflessness and guilt when they failed to meet their own perceptions of how things should be. This opened them up to exploitation. Their desire for respectability left them open to a critical self-examination in which they would always feel themselves to be failing.

Many of the women rejected perceptions of themselves as working class. They felt it to be shameful and equated it with poverty, poor jobs and unemployment, roughness and being common. The women had enrolled on the Caring courses to avoid being seen as working class, to gain employment and to distance themselves from negative perceptions of working-class status. In fact, there was a degree to which they denied class divisions. Furthermore, not only did the women reject class divisions in many cases (unless forced by social circumstance to recognise their position), they also did not fit neatly into the pattern of the Registrar General's account of class which took class status from the employment status of the nearest male relative. Their mothers contributed to household income and were sometimes the main breadwinners.

The desire to reject working-class status led women to a continuous programme of self-improvement that often focused on their bodies. Dress and cosmetics formed an important part of the control and maintenance of a respectable image. Homes were a 'site' for creating a sense of identity and the women commented on their furnishings and homes in such as way to as to display knowledge of middle-class taste and felt the need to apologise for their inability to afford the trappings of what they saw as being somehow superior. This does not mean that they liked the middle classes – many did not and speak disparagingly of the rich and middle-class as being snobbish, badly dressed and mean with money. Although the women rejected class it is central to their lives, as in their very rejection of working-class identity and their investing of so much time and effort in clothing, material goods, leisure pursuits and their homes.

Women have to learn to recognise themselves as being feminine and to develop an idea of what being feminine is. One of the strongest social constructions with a very long historical pedigree is the notion of the 'lady'. A lady is white, middle class, frail, passive and dependent. This is something to which women should aim as it embodies respectability. Working-class women, however, are robust and sexual. The women of Skeggs's study gained pleasure and status from the process of looking good, of mediating between appearing attractive and tarty, or looking feminine and looking sexy. There are dangers for women who somehow get it wrong of being too concerned with appearance or 'letting themselves go'. They are rejected by their peer groups. Desirability is an important part of the meaning of being female, but to be respectable means to subdue sexuality. It is a fine and difficult distinction so women will spend more time investing in their appearance in some situations than others. The function of men then is to give women the confidence of *knowing* that they are desired rather than actually being desired. Undesirable women with no steady relationships are made to feel unvalued in a society that places much esteem on heterosexual partnerships and on marriage.

Women often feel shame at sexuality and their own bodies which are seen as 'not respectable'. Their courses in Caring took marriage and heterosexuality for granted. Indeed, one examination asked students to define the difficulties in choosing a marriage partner and expected in responses to see references to the difficulties of mixed-ethnicity marriage. There are, as Skeggs points out, clear racist and sexist assumptions in this 'knowledge'. To be unmarried represented a form of failure. Flirtation, however, offers a route to power and control for pretty girls – particularly with male teachers – and it is an exchange that is understood. However, the girls also resented their passivity and would indulge in group humiliations of male teachers by making personal and direct references to male anatomy. Some women would distance themselves from such crudity in an effort to maintain respectability, but nevertheless enjoyed the exchanges. Some women experienced real fear of being thought a 'tart', and this extended to expressions of sexual pleasure. Curiously, one woman spent time in gay bars assessing and appraising the sexual attractiveness of the men, an activity that would not be respectable in a straight bar where there would be the danger of sexual approach.

The women of the sample tended to reject feminism and did not recognise it as being relevant to their lives and life experiences. They misunderstood the nature of feminism, equating it with anti-pornography and lesbianism even when they expressed themselves as being dissatisfied with elements of their lives. Some rejected feminism due to their perception of it being 'anti-man'. Feminism had the most meaning for the girl who had to remove herself from an abusive and unpleasant relationship to protect herself and her son.

IMPORTANCE

This is a very important book in the sense that it forms part of a wider sequence of work that Skeggs has undertaken. However, more than that, it looks at the construction of feminine identity in a way that offers a contrast to masculinist thinking. Some postmodernists suggest that gender is becoming optional. This study provides a counter to that argument by showing that gender and class are significant in people's lives and are an important part of the way in which women define their own identities. Moreover, working-class female identity is forged in a struggle for respectability – this is a long-running battle for recognition as being of value as an individual against a culture and an education system that traps them in a sense of guilt and worthlessness.

EVALUATION

This book addresses questions of what it actually means to be a woman in daily life in a way that retrieves the debate from the experiences of the literate middle-classes – who are probably less bound by the demands of being feminine than are working-class women. However, we seem to learn a great deal more about Skeggs and her intellectual journey in the introductory chapters than we do about the women she studied. Given that the claim of the study is to put the experiences of ordinary women at the forefront of the research, it would have been interesting to learn something more about them. Their daily routines, their relationships and their families seem somehow distant, and their individualities fail to develop – despite the fact that their observations on life are so witty and clever. The focus is on class and respectability as a whole and not on the sample.

The analyses take priority over the quotations offered from the women themselves, so there is little exploration of the representativeness of the quotations offered. The picture that Skeggs draws of the women's lives presents a familiar picture. She discusses Friday and Saturday nights out, when women dress well and share jokes and companionship. This leads to a discussion of the view that femininity is a bourgeois concept that is distant from the reality of working-class femininity. However, it would have been interesting to know how frequently group-partying happens, something about the social arrangements leading to it and the attitude of partners towards it. Yet this daily, more mundane element is somehow lost in detail about the deconstruction of the experience's meaning as a collective experience of shared gender. There are also other gaps in the experiences offered to readers. It would have been interesting to know more about male/female relationships, for instance.

Nonetheless, the writer of this book has a clear respect and affection for these women, without over-identifying with them or making them either the heroes or the victims of the narrative. Skeggs has given an academic reality to women who are frequently invisible and disregarded in studies, and offered an insight into their lives and thought. It is a shame that, probably, very few of them will have access to this form of sociological narrative, rooted as it is in the discourses and concerns of the academics.

QUESTIONS

KNOWLEDGE AND UNDERSTANDING

1 Describe the sampling process used by Skeggs.
2 What were the aims of this research?
3 What makes this research typical of feminist research-processes?
4 Why do working-class women value respectability?
5 What value did Caring courses place on the home knowledge that girls brought into the classroom?
6 Why did working-class girls reject working-class status?
7 Why did working-class women feel that feminism was not relevant to them?

ANALYSIS

1 What practical problems did Skeggs face in conducting this study?
2 Attempt to define the features of working-class female notions of respectability.
3 Suggest how you would attempt a similar study to identify how middle-class women gain their notions of what it is to be female.

MARKETING MOLLY AND MELVILLE:
DATING IN A POSTMODERN, CONSUMER SOCIETY

Elizabeth Jagger

'Sociology' Vol 35 no1 February 2001

CONTEXT

The quest for a partner in love or marriage forms a central part of most Western story-telling and literature; especially that produced for women. Given the significance of the heterosexual pair-bonded couple at the centre of social convention, it has probably never been an easy process for people to meet and form permanent relationships. Early advertising for suitable marriage partners can be dated back to the sixteenth century in Britain and to the early 1800s in the USA, when brides could be ordered by men via mail-order catalogues. Many social groups such as European Jews have used a match-maker system to engineer relationships between prospective couples.

In the 1980s, it became socially acceptable in Britain to advertise in magazines and newspapers, or to use the internet in order to make contact with others. Before then, personal self-advertising had been seen as something of a last resort and a point of shame. Social conventions had changed, however, and for many the pressure of work made advertising a viable option in the search for a partner. It is a relatively passive process in that having placed the advertisement, the individual relies on others to respond and this is rather different from face-to-face interaction where there is always the fear of rebuff and rejection. Curiously, Jagger points out, despite the significance and importance of the topic, there is very little in academic literature on this area of social life.

This research was not particularly concerned with the fact of advertising to negotiate the complex social process of meeting a partner, but more with the way in which people use the process of creating an advertisement in order to present an identity that will attract a member of the opposite sex. This is a subtle distinction but an important one. The concern with the creation of one or more self-identities is very much a theme of postmodern research. This means that the research issue in this study is just as interesting as the question of *who* advertises in such a way. In a newspaper advertisement for a friend or partner, one is forced to create an attractive social persona in a very few words. Moreover, this persona has to have some basis in a perceived reality because it functions to attract someone who may wish to form a relationship.

The aims of the research were to:

- investigate the range of meanings that the advertisers attached to gender categories
- examine the extent to which the meanings of the terms 'masculine' and 'feminine' have changed from traditional stereotypes
- investigate whether identities for men and for women have also diversified.

METHODS

We learn very little about the social background of the advertisers or what has led them to advertise. Indeed, there is little discussion at all about the people who created the advertisements. What appears is a postmodern deconstruction of the meaning of the advertisements themselves.

Jagger produced earlier research involving a sample of over a thousand advertisements from two Scottish papers, the *Herald* and the *Scotsman* and two national papers, the *Guardian* and *The Independent*. These are newspapers with a mainly middle-class readership, but the author of the study felt that as the emphasis was on gender and not class this sampling process was not unduly unrepresentative. All four newspapers had similar advertisements and so the presentations of self to be found in the contents of the advertisements were not biased according to the venue the advertiser chose. Advertisements that were rejected from the sample were repeat advertisements, group advertisements and lesbian/gay individuals. The particular reason for rejecting homosexual advertising of either gender was because the researcher felt that it might be difficult to decode the particular language cues that may be used in this type of advertising. The gay community tends to use specific codes that might only be accessible to someone who was part of that social group.

The samples of advertisements were collected over a four-week period in March and May 1996. This was to control for seasonal variations. Although the researcher had access to a large sample, the focus for this particular article consisted of 100 advertisements: 50 composed by males and 50 by females.

KEY FINDINGS

Almost all previous research has noted that males and females conform to their social stereotypes when creating advertisements. Men emphasise education, wealth and status, but women stress attractiveness and physical attributes. Much of this work, however, was conducted within the framework of evolutionary psychology (biological determinism) which suggests that men offer financial standing and security, while women offer a caring nature and a pretty face and figure because this is related to their differing investments in reproduction. Other psychologists have linked the descriptions of advertisers to personality traits or to the idea that advertisers are developing advertisements that suit the traits that the opposite gender requires of a mate. The findings, however, remain similar and locked in the understanding that gender is itself an unchanging quantity. This means that the studies were not located in any particular location, culture or time-frame.

There has been a detailed literature of contemporary social change in Britain, much of it located within postmodernist debates. It is claimed by a number of writers that identities derive less from our occupations and more from our patterns of consumption. The development of an identity is a choice, or a personal project. This, Jagger claims, means that the nature of self-advertising is now linked to issues of body and lifestyle resources for both genders. It is this last point that she set out to test with her study.

Jagger claims that a 'more limited number of identities are available for women relative to men'. Gender stereotyping is a feature of such advertising so that half of the female adverts samples emphasis physical attractiveness and caring and nurturing capacities. Many mentioned being slim and petite. Those who could not claim slim offered 'cuddly' . The body therefore was offered as an object of pleasure and in some cases the advertisers referred to themselves in overtly sexual terms: 'sensual' or 'sensuous'. Jagger argues that many of the advertisers refer to themselves almost only in terms of describing the body. The interesting point that she notes is that approximately a third of women offered a view of themselves as 'independent' or 'professional'. Some, however, temper the image of professional career women with stereotypical female imagery; one female describes herself as both 'graduate' and 'sensuous'. Other women describe themselves as not just bodies for pleasure, but bodies that are disciplined, so sport and fitness are mentioned. Jagger reads this in terms of professional women who are in control of their lives rather than offering beauty as being submission.

One feature of female self-advertising involves references to literature or popular culture. One example cited refers to *Les Miserables*, for instance, and another has a number of romantic filmic references. This is read by Jagger as being ironic and humorous, which it is; note that in the evaluation, however, alternative and more pragmatic readings are possible for this device of the advertiser. Jagger notes that other women challenge stereotypical femininity through parody and exaggeration. This allows them to challenge male superiority and sometimes offer sexuality without the need to progress to a pair-bonded relationship.

Men offer a far more varied account of themselves than women. A third of the men mentioned occupational or educational status. These men tended to emphasise conventional male images of themselves as thinkers. Others, however, offered lifestyle and sexiness. Jagger fails to note whether there is an age difference between the two groups and it would be interesting to note whether younger men offer different self-images from older men. The life-stylers tended to refer to themselves in terms of body shape; slimness being a feature of their self-imaging. Some men referred to their bodies in terms of their outdoor interests and they tended to claim masculine sports such as hill-walking and skiing for themselves.

A number of 'new men' were apparent in the advertisements. They mentioned themselves as 'supportive' or 'caring'. These men offer relationships and some even mention that single parents would be acceptable partners. These are viewed by Jagger as 'liberated versions of masculine selfhood'. In contrast, there are a number of 'lads' who advertise, often in terms that are derogatory of women but which are funny and ironic. The advertisers depict themselves in terms that are typically male, mentioning football, pubs and seeking women who are variously a 'bimbo', an 'erotic nymphomaniac' and 'voluptuous'. A further small group of men emphasised New Age characteristics. They talk of themselves as 'spiritual' or 'rugged'. The term 'eco-type' occurred. These males are concerned with presenting themselves as rather disembodied and introspective.

In conclusion, Jagger notes that there has been an increase in the type and variety of images that people can construct for themselves. There are far more male identities available than female, however. There has been a proliferation of male self-images, but females are more restricted in their self-created identities. Female identities tend to be reworkings of older identities and women still are unable to resist the pressure of appealing to the male gaze.

IMPORTANCE One of the most interesting and significant observations made in the article is that males are tending to look away from their occupations to gain a sense of identity. They describe themselves in terms of their personalities. In contrast, women are beginning to identify themselves in terms of work and professional status. This may be one of the futures of the study of gender, the way in which there have been shifts in gendered behaviours. This study also challenges the commonly held view of many postmodernists that gender distinctions are becoming blurred. It shows that while change is happening, distinctions between male and female self-image are still significant and strongly held. Although it is operating within postmodern conventions and styles of thought, this study issues a serious challenge to the conclusions of postmodernist analysis.

EVALUATION

Jagger is not concerned with drawing a cross-section of the population who advertise. Her concern is purely with the mechanics of created gendered identities. This is valid and understandable in terms of her viewpoint. However, the point here is that the advertising is analysed in isolation. We do not learn what percentage of males stipulates that the responding females should be slim. We learn little of whether more males than females advertise. If both genders are advertising in equal numbers then socially constructed identities reflect the whims of the advertiser. However, if one gender is in rather more short supply than another or one gender is more likely to be seeking sex while the other requires love, a whole different set of social dynamics come into play in terms of what the advertiser will stress. This is actually a very significant point, because we therefore do not learn to what extent advertisements by males for females affect what the females say about themselves, or vice versa.

Jagger notes that other studies do not take account of location, space and time but this is a criticism that could equally well be made of this study. We have no historical evidence of advertising in previous years to act as a control against this sample. As a result it is impossible to see whether the purpose of the advertisement was for a long-term companion or a short-term sexual flirtation or to judge whether the social background of advertisers has changed. We cannot even tell which adverts gain responses or are successful in attracting the correct responses. To a certain extent, we have to take it on trust that more and different varieties of gender typing are offered compared with the advertising of the past.

Some of the conclusions and observations hardly seem to be as surprising or as significant as the author appears to think. The fact of a third of females describing themselves as being 'professional' or 'independent' would not be surprising given the venue for the advertising. The *Guardian* is not noted as a newspaper for the ill-educated and given that it has supplements for secretarial and office work, education and social work on various days of the week, it must be a paper which is popular with the feminised professions! Similarly, the *Independent* is well read by those in public-service sectors which are also heavily weighted towards female employment. The article tends to offer readings and explanations of points that are supported not by empirical data or triangulation with research into advertisers or commentary on social context, but with references to theoretical writing by other commentators. This is sociology that is more interested in theory than in the behaviour of ordinary people.

Alternative readings are possible for some of the examples used. For instance, complex filmic references may not be intended as a deliberate self-imaging for an ironic postmodern female who is offering a view of herself and 'reflexive, critical, segregated from the old language of sexual prescriptions'. It may operate as a simple device to screen out males who would not understand or share the interests of the female.

Curiously, Jagger notes the euphemism 'cuddly' to describe those who cannot call themselves slim but omits to comment on other words that carry a similar implication in the wording of the adverts that she cites: 'curvaceous' may carry the implication of flesh. 'Rubensesque' (sic) is another example; the painter Rubens was famous for enjoying painting women who were rather fat by modern standards of beauty.

The 'new man' of the advertisements may not in fact be new males but newer versions of old stereotypes. These advertisers may be men who are seeking a wife and who recognise that being recognisable as good husband and father material is a way of attaining this end. The paternal male who looks after his woman is hardly a new version of masculinity.

QUESTIONS

KNOWLEDGE AND UNDERSTANDING

1. Describe the sampling process used by Jagger.
2. What were the aims of this research?
3. Why did self-advertising become respectable in the 1980s?
4. What forms of female identity are offered in the advertisements?
5. What forms of male identity are offered in the adverts?
6. Why did Jagger study self-advertisements?

ANALYSIS

1. How representative of self-advertising was Jagger's sampling process?
2. How representative of possible gender identities was Jagger's sampling process?
3. Suggest ethical and practical reasons why it might be difficult to contact self-advertisers.
4. How far do you feel that Jagger was able to achieve her all of her aims?

WOMEN, VIOLENCE AND MALE POWER

Edited by Marianne Hester, Liz Kelly and Jill Radford

Open University Press, Buckingham, 1996

CONTEXT

This is a book that wears its feminist heart with some pride. Even on the cover, the word 'violence' is emboldened away from the rest of the title. The main research-interest of each of the contributors involves abuse, rape and violence against women and children.

The history of feminism is chequered. While individual women have been arguing for better rights for women for generations, these were often individuals from relatively wealthy and privileged backgrounds. Feminism probably only became a major force relatively recently and it has always been marked by controversy and media misrepresentation. Radical feminists have accused males of being rapists and equally there has been a backlash against feminists so that they are represented as being sexually unattractive and bitter. In fact, feminism consists of rather more than the public perception of the debate allows for. There are, for example, methodological issues. Feminist research is qualitative and experiential, which means that researchers will refer to their own personal experiences. This leads to a concern with the minute detail of individual lives, with families, gender and sexuality. There is also an interest in the nature of power itself, as it is expressed through patriarchy.

Feminist research dating from the 1960s and 1970s showed that men used violence against women and that this violence had a sexual connotation in that these men found the exercise of power against women to be a 'turn on'. This was a shocking revelation at a time when domestic violence was a matter of shame for the female victim who was commonly seen to have initiated it in some way because of her own behaviour. Once women felt able to discuss their experiences, a whole new dimension of family life became open for researchers. There is little doubt that while feminism has been presented as an object of humour in many quarters, the observations made by women have had a powerful effect on social policy. The treatment of children and female victims of violence by the police, for instance, has undergone a radical change which makes the system a little easier to use, but which, according to the authors, has not gone far enough in accepting female experiences as valid experiences.

The editors of this book take feminist debate one step further by taking account of the criticism of mainstream feminism that was made by black feminists. Black feminists suggested that much feminism was white and middle class, and therefore did not take account of the experiences of black and working-class women. This understanding has brought new elements to the discussion. The editors therefore point out that women themselves may use violence. They do, however, reassert that most, if not all women, have at some time experienced violence, harassment and abuse from men.

METHODS

There is very little discussion of the methods used by the researchers who are all members of the Violence Against Women Study Group. They set themselves up at the time of the British Sociological Association conference on War, Violence and Social Change in 1985. This informal and flexible group of women meet regularly and come from across the UK. It is a forum for political campaigning so that it has made representations on laws and legal practice as they relate to violent men or women who have killed violent partners.

The aims of the book were to:

- update an earlier book *Women, Violence and Social Control* (1987) which consisted of papers from the conference
- develop a further understanding of the ways in which differences between different groups of women affected their experience of violence.

To understand the methods used, it is necessary to refer to theoretical perspectives used by various feminists. The best known of the radical feminists were Shulasmith Firestone (1970) and Kate Millet (1971), who saw the 'personal as political'. They claimed that women are just as oppressed in their homes as they are in the economic world. This position has been refined through debate and discussion so that feminist research can be identified by the following characteristics.

1. The researcher should identify and empathise with the subjects of the study.
2. Research should focus on the oppressed – in this case, women and their children.
3. Research should be political and aim for the emancipation of women.
4. Research should examine the world from the perspective of women.
5. Research should be carried out by the victims of oppression, women.
6. Women's personal experiences should be documented to rescue them from the 'invisibility' they experience in 'malestream' writing.
7. Research should be shared and open to all women in order to retrieve it from male domination.
8. There is a heavy emphasis on personal experience, participant observation, unstructured interviewing, the use of diaries and observations.

KEY FINDINGS

Each of the chapters offers a different set of findings and so a short summary of some of the most interesting or significant is offered. Each one chosen will be listed under the chapter heading and the author/s.

'NOTHING REALLY HAPPENED': Liz Kelly and Jill Radford

The argument here is that women are often encouraged to be silent about abuse they experience from men. This is a complex process in which the masculine nature of language and social processes becomes exposed. An act is only a crime if it breaks the law. As laws are made by men, certain behaviours that distress women are not criminalised. Examples are drawn from a community study in Wandsworth and the behaviours described by respondents were clearly upsetting and threatening, but not criminal. Kerb-crawling, abuse, comments from male strangers, intimidation by groups of boys and men formed part of daily experience. Within the workspace, women had experienced harassment, sexually based racial remarks and offensive comments that are explained away by men as 'joking'. Within the home they experienced sexual groping and innuendo which were unpleasan, but not provable as criminal. When women say 'nothing happened' they mean, whatever it was, it could have been worse. When the law says 'nothing happened', that is what it means.

'WHEN DOES SPEAKING PROFIT US?': Liz Kelly
Women are encouraged to be silent by men. They do not discuss their experiences, believing them to be of no significance. This paper was designed to challenge women by discussing the violence of women – in particular, lesbians. This is an area of profound concern because it may challenge feminist assumptions that females are the victims of patriarchy. However, some violence may be a response to feelings of powerlessness, so that female violence to men is often a response to experiencing abuse oneself or as a result of it occurring towards one's children. Lesbian violence therefore may be a response to insecurity whereas male violence is prompted by feelings of ownership. Female sexual abusers of children often acted at the prompting of a male partner.

'READING DANGER': Elizabeth Stanko
This chapter is concerned with the way that men and women perceive sexually harassing behaviour. Females often report sexual harassment, only to find that their harassers claim that their behaviour was mere joking, misunderstood or simply did not occur as the woman stated it did. The writer herself reflects on her own experience and yet remains unable to fully describe details despite recalling the emotions with great clarity. The case was protracted, public and chased through a legal process that resulted in an apology from the abuser. Sexual harassment has been a feature of male–female workplace relations for years. The change is that women now resist it; however, the individual who does resist is engaged in individual defiance of the routines of society and is challenged on a number of fronts including her sexuality and her medical and sexual history. Training films and guidance materials do not address issues of patriarchy and the abuse of women; they focus, instead, on what the woman can do to protect herself. There is a tension, however, in the fact that not all women interpret sexualised behaviour as harassment, some are flattered by it. The public pressure is on women to stop claiming sexual harassment rather than on men to stop doing it.

'CONTRADICTIONS AND COMPROMISES': Marianne Hester and Lorraine Radford
This is a study of the impact of the Children Act of 1989 (enforced 1991) on family life where divorce has taken place subsequent to male violence towards the wife. It is claimed that the Children Act reinforces traditional ideologies of family life and family values. At a time when many other government policies were supporting the victims of domestic abuse, this particular Act undermined those intentions. The 1989 Act was designed to emphasise the rights of the child, and included in their rights is the right to have access to both parents. In a series of interviews with lawyers, it was discovered that violence is not taken into account when court orders for parental access are made. Professionals see mothers as obstructive towards the father's rights to see a child. Mothers, however, are concerned that their children are at risk of violence from the father and see professional social workers and courts as being unaware of safety issues. It was often the risk of violence towards the children that prompted them to leave unsatisfactory marriages in the first case. Women can be controlled by men, and even experience continued violence at their hands subsequent to divorce, through access orders to their children. In cases of custody being challenged, abusive males have accused wives of being poor mothers for moving into places of refuge while their own violence is not considered a relevant argument.

'UNREASONABLE DOUBT': Sue Lees
There is little research into the workings of the legal system in relation to violence against women. It is difficult to gain access to official records or to gain funding for such research. What is clear is that many women have experienced rape and very few report it, despite the attempts of the police to make the process of reporting rape less intimidating and aggressive towards the victim. Having reported a rape, it is

still very difficult to get a conviction. Cases that fail after reporting has taken place fail for the following reasons.

1 They are not recorded as crimes by the police. Reasons for this include withdrawal by the complainant after further threats of violence or because the police thought the females were making false allegations.
2 The police downgrade cases so that a complaint of rape becomes redefined as indecent assault. One particularly brutal case where a victim was slashed across the breasts and penetrated was downgraded to GBH.
3 The Crown Prosecution Service will only recommend a case if they feel that there is likely to be a conviction. This is difficult in many rape cases.
4 The court process rarely convicts men of rape even in cases of multiple attacks. The defence will attack a complaining woman's morality, reliability, sexual history and general truthfulness. Juries may also be misdirected and confused by legal arguments.

Sue Lees then points out that in her view, the legal process is the equivalent of a second rape for women. It legitimises male violence and is a 'mockery of justice'.

IMPORTANCE

This series of studies is fascinating though some men may find it uncomfortable reading. It is a mistake to think that because some men and a masculine social system prejudices social life against women this means all men are abusers. This, however, understates the complexity of the case. Clearly men require some re-education and understanding of the harm many of them do to women as a result of ignorance and lack of understanding. We have a portrait here of a social system that is adjusting to the claims of women to be treated as equals and that is allowing them unprecedented freedom in the workplace and home without fully addressing the issues of male power and violence that restrict them and make them fearful. Women are pointing out real gendered injustices, and feminism is essential part of that process. This book is not just about equal pay (significant though that is to females) it is also about the way that social life and experience for many women is defined by male violence or the threat that it presents.

EVALUATION

While some of the methods used by feminist sociologists are open to accusations of being deliberately political and value-laden, nevertheless it is clear that much of the material describing the nature of women's experiences would not have been obtained through any other methods. Silence and an unwillingness to discuss issues surrounding abuse, patriarchy and male violence are typical of female reactions. Men misunderstand or do not interpret behaviours in the same way that women do. Whilst this is not a new perception, being both the stuff of regular public-media discussion and of comedy, it is always worth recalling the important point that it is men who define the world and women who must live according to parameters that they have not set.

There must be concerns with any perspective that sees femininity alone as being victimised. Gender issues affect males and they too can be victims of the social construction of masculinity to which males and females must subscribe. Although female voices deserve to be heard, this text, while cool in tone, is based upon anger at injustice. There is a justifiable support for the perception that women are not fully considered by those with the power to respond to the complaints of feminists. This book was written by women, for women and about women. It is certainly fully political in intent. How effective it will be as a political weapon until the jokes at the expense of feminism cease remains an interesting question that students will have to answer for themselves.

In the focus on the daily experience of women, there is a slight lack of balance and there are, perhaps, too few reminders of the significance of institutional sexism and racism on groups of women, although their impact on individual experience is well discussed.

QUESTIONS

KNOWLEDGE AND UNDERSTANDING

1 Why do feminists consider it necessary to study women separately from men?
2 What were the aims of this book?
3 Summarise the main characteristics of feminist research.
4 Suggest reasons why feminist researchers tend to reject empiricism and scientific approaches to sociology.
5 Why do feminists believe that 'female silence' is an important tool of patriarchal oppression?
6 Why has there been little research into the workings of the legal system with regard to male violence against women? Develop your answer with reference to all of the studies mentioned.
7 Use your own sociological knowledge and experience of the study of gender to suggest ways in which men can be the victims of the social construction of masculinity.

ANALYSIS

1 What problems of reliability do researchers in the feminist tradition face in conducting a study?
2 Are studies of one gender alone justified in the light of our present sociological understandings of the nature of sexism?
3 Evaluate the suggestion that sociology should be political and value-laden in intent.

References Firestone, S (1972), *The Dialectics of Sex*, Paladin, London
Hanmer, J and Maynard, M (1987), Women, Violence and Social Control, Macmillan, Basingstoke
Millett, K (1970), *Sexual Politics*, Doubleday, New York

A STUDY OF TOWN LIFE:
LIVING STANDARDS IN THE CITY OF YORK 100 YEARS AFTER ROWNTREE

Meg Huby, Jonathan Bradshaw and Anne Corden

Joseph Rowntree Foundation, York, 1999

CONTEXT

One of the earliest and most significant studies into poverty was conducted by Seebohm Rowntree in his native city of York in 1899. This research has become the starting point for many discussions of poverty since that date. His choice of York as a place of study was not merely for reasons of convenience but also because it was a fairly typical town, not dissimilar to many others in Britain at that time. The more recent study of York in this book was designed both to commemorate Rowntree's initial pioneering work and to update it with a view of the City of York as it is today.

York is an extremely pretty and pleasant city. It has heritage status and attracts visitors from the whole world. It appears on the surface to be affluent – there are pleasant suburbs around a lovely historic centre full of museums, eating places and expensive shops. Nevertheless, the attractive surface of the city means that social problems are hidden away from the public surface. One of the aims of this study is to discover the extent of social problems associated with deprivation in the modern City of York.

The city that Rowntree studied is not the same City of York today. This is not an observation on the fact that times and social conditions have changed (which they obviously have) but a comment on administrative changes that mean that the area now denoted as City of York is larger than that of Rowntree's day. These administrative changes, dating from the mid-1990s, have resulted in an increase in the numbers of employers and middle-class professions and a decrease in the numbers of workers. The modern city has more dual-income families than the national average, while percentages of unemployed people over the age of 55 has reduced slightly. The number of children living in households with no earning adults stood at 12.1% in 1999, which is below the national average.

Modern York itself has a larger population than old City of York. General population changes mean that, since Rowntree's time, the numbers of elderly people have increased and these form a higher proportion of the population than they once did. There has also been an increase in lone-parent families and in women who work outside the home. There has been a decline in traditional industry and a growth in the service sector. Congestion is a problem and there is pressure on public spaces and leisure facilities. As the authors of the report point out, the results of such changes are experienced differently by different social groups.

METHODS

One of Seebohm Rowntree's major achievements was to attempt to define and measure poverty. This he did in terms of the income necessary to maintain a basic but healthy standard of living. His approach was radical at the time, but understandings since Rowntree's day have changed. While Rowntree used absolute measures of poverty, focusing on food, shelter and warmth, few people would find his measure acceptable today. Modern commentators on poverty tend to use relative notions of poverty, which rely on the understanding that poverty can mean a lack of things that a society deems as essential for living. In addition, the notion of social exclusion – being shut out of key aspects of social and community life – is gaining currency.

In the absence of a clear lead from government data, many local authorities have developed their own data sources for attempting to establish the extent of poverty in Britain. The authors are aware of these studies; nonetheless, the modern study began by defining poverty in terms of life chances and lifestyle. Certain groups are likely to experience low income: the elderly, the young, those of minority ethnic groups, and the sick or disabled. The researchers then located these groups within administrative areas and attempted to study life-style and life chances in terms of geographical location. They note that while an area may be deprived, not all of those who live within it experience deprivation. Note, however, that living in a poor area will itself have a negative impact on people's life chances because of limited health and education facilities.

Two types of data were collected.

1 **Qualitative data** was collected by conducting semi-structured interviews with representatives of community bodies such as churches and community groups. Meetings were held throughout the City of York so that a range of residents was consulted. The large research team also commissioned reports and writing that reviewed people's personal experiences of disadvantage.
2 **Quantitative data** was collected using secondary materials such as the 1991 Census, council figures and data from other public bodies such as the Benefits Agency, Health Service and hospitals. In addition, a sample survey was conducted to establish the prevalence of poverty. We have very limited details of this survey: neither the questions nor the sampling procedures are discussed fully in this report.

KEY FINDINGS

Each of the chapters provided offers a summary of city life with reference to social problems and experience of life in the city for its residents.

EMPLOYMENT

British society has experience of very rapid changes in employment structure since the end of World War II and York is no exception to this. There has been a loss of manufacturing employment and an expansion in service-sector employment. This is not necessarily good news, however, because the impact of this social change on employment in the City of York has been to create a rapid decline in the number of men in full-time work. Service-sector work has been expanding, and this social development has provided some with opportunities for high-status occupations and a comfortable life-style. However, the majority of service-sector workers are employed in part-time, insecure, poorly paid and undemanding jobs in food outlets and shops. Declining levels in male employment has been accompanied by increasing levels of female work. This has led to an increase in poverty as female workers in York earn 15% below the national average whereas men earn 7.3% below national average earnings. Ten per cent of workers were earning less than £165.10p a week, though Family Credit would add a further £42.51 if the worker were a man with a non-working wife and two dependent children.

Job opportunities were limited so that the majority of posts on offer were for part-time or casual work offering rates of pay that were less than £50 a week. The jobs were not suitable for a main income-earner needing to support a family or for a single parent to earn enough to pay for childcare. The local Citizens Advice Bureau received numerous complaints about job security and employment rights or low pay. In 1997, men were working for hourly rates of significantly less than £3.00 an hour. Many community groups felt this to be placing unacceptable strain on family relationships and health. In addition, in 1997, there were over 3,000 long-term unemployed people in York. Nearly 25% of these people were under 24.

WELFARE BENEFITS

Of the population of York, 7.2% were drawing Income Support and 14.6% of children were eligible for full school meals. These are not exceptional figures, but even in a relatively affluent city such as York, it is surprising to see that one in six children required food subsidy of this sort. Advice and information centres about benefits tended to be located within the city centre, but those who required the advice usually lived in outlying council estates and there had been a reduction in funding of services resulting in the withdrawal of a bus service offering advice to claimants.

EDUCATION

In 1997, 50 children left school without qualifications. This seems to be a low figure, which ties in with the perception that York is a relatively wealthy city with pockets of poverty and deprivation. High percentages of children had been identified as having special needs, but very low numbers of these had legal statements of special educational needs. This suggests that there was unwillingness at some point in the education system to provide children with statements because these carry with them legal rights for parents and funding implications for schools. Exclusions from York schools 'fell from 502 in 1995–96 to 377 in 1996–97'. In 1997, 34 students were permanently excluded.

RISK OF POVERTY

Twenty per cent of the population of York were over retirement age. Elderly people were particularly vulnerable to poverty and many of their income resources were taken up by ill-health, inappropriate accommodation or need for services and care. As part of a rationalisation and cost-cutting exercise in 1997 the council was increasing its fees for services such as hot-meal deliveries or domestic help. Disability figures suggested that a large proportion of the population experience disability. Support groups for the blind were able to offer estimated figures for those with sight impairment and MIND, a mental-health charity, pointed out that many carers were themselves disabled or frail elderly. Children and young people were vulnerable to living in low-income homes. 12% of the children of York lived in non-earning households. Many of those claiming benefit were aged between 18 and 24. Lone parents were likely to experience poverty, and York had a higher proportion of single parents than many similar districts in England. Access to affordable childcare was limited. York had very low levels of membership of minority ethnic groups; however, unemployment figures were far higher for these groups than resident white populations.

LIVING STANDARDS

Living standards in York appeared to be relatively satisfactory, although 20% of homes had no central heating. There were problems in the rented sector in that many young people claiming housing benefit had their income reduced because rents were considered to be too high. There were some travelling families, approximately 100 in all, and they felt excluded from the social life of the community. Homelessness among young people was a problem and many households were in temporary accommodation due to low income. Church groups provided soup for the homeless and estimated that at least 20 people used its services nightly. Even though York was well supported with charities and agencies, significant numbers of people appeared to be 'trapped in destitution'. Women in York were particularly vulnerable to crime and many experienced abusive relationships. Drugs were easy to obtain and relatively cheap compared with the prices for alcohol. Drug abusers tended to be young, and drink-abuse by young people was also seen as a problem. There was widespread experience of debt, and evictions, home repossession and high rents contributed to problems. Many people relied on public transport but the city was also encouraging the use of bicycles. There was wide provision of art, but most people saw artistic enterprise as being the province only of the wealthy.

IMPORTANCE This research looks at the impact of recent social and political change on the life of a community and points to areas of real concern. Employment is targeted as one area where poverty is created by social policy. Despite the fact that York has good welfare services and a variety of voluntary bodies, these are not working together to support the lives of the most vulnerable members of the community. A portrait is drawn of an attractive and vibrant community that is failing its weakest members. This may be a pattern that can be generalised to much of British society.

EVALUATION

Although this study is about the experience of poverty in the City of York, the voices of the poor are curiously missing, whilst church and community group leaders and organisers are constantly referred to. Clearly, the research team spoke to large numbers of groups and organisations. However, there is a problem in terms of validity in this approach because social-exclusion theory suggests that many of the poorest people will not perhaps participate fully in the lives of their community. One should always have very strong reservations about which client groups these church leaders actually represent if figures cited in the secularisation debates are to be trusted!

There is a somewhat surprising lack of sense of place in this study given that it is based on a particular community at one particular point in time. Many of the observations are so general as to be of no particular interest or insight to anyone. A brief overview of the welfare-benefit system is followed by the observation that few claimants understand the system and that people have difficulty accessing information. Although interestingly, this is explained in terms of the withdrawal of a bus advisory service, on the whole a lack of local politics and information dulls the report. We learn that many single parents received gifts of food and support counselling at Christmas but search in vain for actual census data to find out just how many people actually do live in the city. There is also a lack of context against national figures so that we learn for instance that 8.5% of residents of York had a degree or higher degree without reference to whether this is actually better or worse than national figures. The data is presented in a general vacuum that makes it difficult for an average reader to understand the full context of the picture of the city that is proffered.

The authors of the report carefully avoid drawing conclusions from their work, so a dramatic fall in exclusions from school is noted without any supporting explanation to account for the change. This approach was one of the stated aims of the authors of the study, who attempted to describe the problem rather than explore solutions. Nevertheless, this makes the researchers seem distant from their topic. Education commentators know that a number of social and political factors may come into play in terms of exclusion data and that some schools exclude far more than others. Exclusion data is political data and commentary would have added understanding of the implications of the raw figures.

Overall, the report will be of serious interest to those involved in social policy and service provision. Town planners and those interested in social administration will also find it a fascinating document. This is because it offers a picture of an active community with wide-ranging services and a committed group of community leaders who nevertheless feel that large numbers of people are falling through the net of social-security provision due to low incomes and poor job prospects. As an updating of the portrait of the city described by Seebohm Rowntree this study follows in a long tradition of analysing the community of York and will be useful as a baseline for service provision for future study.

QUESTIONS

KNOWLEDGE AND UNDERSTANDING

1 What was significant about Seebohm Rowntree's study of York in 1899?
2 How has York changed since that date?
3 Summarise some of the changes that have happened in broader society since 1899.
4 How have notions of poverty changed since 1899?
5 How have changes in employment pattern contributed to poverty in the City of York?
6 What difficulties are there in determining the extent and experience of poverty among disabled people in York?
7 Who is poor in modern York?

ANALYSIS

1 What are the implications for this research on government policy? Suggest a variety of approaches as to how governments could tackle issues of poverty and inequality in British society using the findings of this research.
2 Suggest reasons why it is important for local authorities to have empirical studies of significant social problems.
3 How might you set about designing a qualitative study of deprivation and poverty in York?

References Rowntree, S (1901), *Poverty: a Study of Town Life*, Macmillan, London

BREADLINE BRITAIN IN THE 1990S

David Gordon and Christina Pantazis (eds)

Ashgate Publishing, Aldershot, 1997

CONTEXT

The study of poverty and inequality are very important in sociology and there have been many small-scale research projects that have tackled such issues. However, in political terms, poverty has become 'invisible' over the past twenty years, with many politicians ignoring it or making public pronouncements suggesting that it no longer exists in modern Britain. Compared with standards of living even thirty years ago, people are generally better dressed, have good leisure facilities and more comfortable homes. However, Gordon and Pantazis suggest that although governments have lost interest in poverty, the general population share a number of views about its nature and significance that are being overlooked by their leaders. Poverty is a problem in modern Britain and many people live in its shadow or in fear of it.

Politically, attitudes to poverty have split into two time-segments since World War II. After the War, and for the next thirty years or so, poverty was considered an evil that must be dealt with. As a result, although poverty persisted, there was discussion of social issues associated with it, and poverty studies were significant and famous. Most of the major studies of poverty date to the 1960s and mid-1970s. As a result of these attitudes, incomes for the poor rose in line with those of the general population. With the advent of the New Right and Thatcherism in 1979, a new approach to the question of poverty arose which suggested that poverty no longer existed in Britain. Concern with the poor faded from the political agenda. Meanwhile, there was a growth in low-paid-sector work and controls on public expenditure and taxation. As a result, there has been a widening in the differentials between the poorest and the richest over the past twenty years, although general standards of living have increased for all. Note that the findings described in this study relate to the policies of the then existing Conservative governments and do not examine later Labour government policies. It pre-dates minimum-wage legislation, for instance. Many have argued, however, that the Labour Party have not so much challenged previous policy thinking, as adopted and adapted it.

METHODS

This book refers to the findings of two different surveys, one conducted in 1983 and a second in 1990. The surveys were conducted by the opinion-polling organisation MORI (Market and Opinion Research International) for two television series made for London Weekend Television. Funding was provided by London Weekend Television and the Joseph Rowntree Foundation. There are references to the evidence presented by respondents in the television series, although clearly this deep study stands on its own as a book written for those with an understanding of the topic rather than as a piece of campaigning journalism (as the programmes probably were).

The aims of the study were to:

- offer some account of the living conditions of the poorest sectors of the community
- examine debates around poverty and the findings of the research team as published in the television series.

One of the most significant debates in this book relates to the very serious question of how to operationalise the concept of poverty. Is it to be defined in terms of actual expenditure and what can be purchased, as the earliest researchers suggested; or, is it a relative concept to be measured in terms of what the general population can expect to earn or own in relation to a set of basic needs as defined by a researcher? The radical solution used by the research team was to define poverty in terms of what the general public considered to be minimum need. This method has since been used by other researchers into poverty.

MORI interviewed a quota sample of 1,174 adults in 1983 and 1,831 adults in 1990. Samples were based on housing types and geographical locations rather than on social groupings. The respondents were asked a sequence of questions about 'possessions and activities'. If more than 50% of the sample considered that an item or activity was essential, then it was considered to be a 'socially perceived necessity'. Later in the questionnaire, the respondents were asked to determine whether the same list of items fitted into a series of categories such as ' Have and could do without' or 'Have and couldn't do without'. Items that respondents said that they 'Don't have and can't afford' but that were considered to be a necessity by over 50% of respondents, registered on a deprivation index.

Much of the rest of the book refers to statistical and economic debates about poverty. There is a complex analysis of its own process of producing a working definition of poverty. The conclusion must be that not only is empirical data on poverty difficult to collect, it is also difficult to analyse effectively and must be supplemented by factual and statistical data produced by official bodies. The study therefore refers widely to official statistics produced by the government itself to produce a damning indictment of the levels of poverty and deprivation in modern Britain. This makes it a difficult book to read, because it requires some understanding of social administration and social policy as well as a concern with the detail of data collation.

KEY FINDINGS

Just as the Conservative governments of the 1980s were beginning to argue that poverty no longer existed in Britain, there was a rise in homelessness and begging that gave the very public lie to this claim. It was unusual to see the destitute in pre-1979 Britain, although they certainly existed in large numbers. The nature of the begging changed too, so that the young homeless became conspicuous in city centres.

There was a degree of fluctuation in poverty. Many households were 'never poor', some 'always poor' but many experienced 'sometimes poor'. This meant that a large number of households who were not currently poor had experienced poverty in the very recent past. Poverty is therefore not a consistent or permanent state, but a fluctuating and transitional phase for many people. Many people are placed on or near the breadline, so that they are not wholly poor, but nonetheless experience deprivation. An example could be the pensioner with a good television, but limited heating and, perhaps, no TV licence.

There is a consistent and persistent body of opinion that suggests that the poor somehow spend their money badly – for example, on drink and cigarettes. This type of thinking underlies much government policy-making. Government statistics suggest, however, that poor households spend considerably less on such luxuries than other households. In fact they spend less on everything. By 1990, only 20% of the British population still subscribed to this point of view, a drop of 23% over 20 years. It is suggested that this is because a large proportion of the population had direct or indirect experience of poverty and were unwilling to blame the victims for their own misfortune. There was a correlation between political allegiance and opinion so that Conservative voters were significantly more likely to blame the poor for poverty than to consider it to be the result of social injustice.

Between 1983 and 1990, there were changes in what the public considered to be a necessity. As standards of living rose, so did the numbers of people considering various items such as a fridge or a telephone to be a necessity. Rises in the numbers considering items to be a necessity rose for all social classes between those two years, with the exception of cigarettes, which the very deprived were more likely than all other social classes to consider a necessity. This is unsurprising given that some research has suggested that the stresses associated with poverty reinforce the addiction in poor people. Plotted against all expenditure on leisure and luxury in all social classes, the poor spent less on cigarette smoking than other social classes on hobbies and activities. Giving up smoking would not stop the poor from being poor, but would lead to better health. Public perceptions of poverty suggested in 1990 that the government was doing too little to tackle deprivation. Over 70% of the sample agreed with this statement. There was an increase in the number willing to accept increases in taxation provided it went to support initiatives for the poor.

Poverty is a gender issue. Females were significantly more likely to be poor than males if they were the heads of households. It was not known how poor women were within households that were headed by men, or if the income was divided equally between partners. Female lone-parents were more likely to be poor than male lone-parents. Older females were more likely to be poor than older males because of the lack of pensions and poor state benefits. Women were more likely to consider food items and expenditure on children to be a necessity, whereas males considered items such as holidays and dishwashers to be essential.

The poor lived anxious lives and were more likely to fear crime than other people. This is reasonable since they are also more likely to be the victims of crime. Victimisation is often linked to poor housing conditions, and the poor may be uninsured or under-insured – so increased fear of crime among the poor is also linked to the impact that crime will have on their lives. There was a link between poverty and disability and long-term sickness. Deprivation can be a cause of sickness and mental ill-health among the poor as they also experience depression, isolation and anxiety. This means that many people who are economically deprived suffer on other indices of deprivation so that they are inclined to be unwell, housing is poor, there is poor take-up of social service provision or they experience disability.

IMPORTANCE

This report draws a series of conclusions about the life of modern Britain that are very difficult to reconcile with a view of a classless society. They will be of key interest to those concerned with the battle to attempt a definition and measurement of poverty. It should fuel debate on public policy and its implications for the poor for a number of years and provide a baseline for further future study into the economics of the most deprived households.

In addition, it draws a picture of a Britain far distant from the reassuring image we see reflected in the media and in political debate and reflects the struggles of many ordinary British people to maintain a semblance of self-respect against the dangers of low pay and insecure employment.

EVALUATION

We have very little information about the quota-sampling process and so can make few judgements about either the validity or the representativeness of the information offered. In fact, given the damning picture that emerges of a divided nation, it may even be that the samples are a little small to justify the conclusions. This means that there is a heavy reliance on official statistics with all the advantages and drawbacks that these entail for sociological research. The actual meaning of poverty for people who experience it is underplayed; on the other hand, this is not necessarily a weakness because the government is condemned by both the survey results and by the information that they themselves provide.

This survey has opened out the debate as to what constitutes poverty and the various problems that exist in its definition. It clearly links poverty and measures of poverty to a social construction based on attitudes, rather than to any economic measure such as a 'breadline' or 'poverty line' as used by previous surveys. It moves away from providing a definition of poverty as defined by a researcher. However, the use of a closed questionnaire still limits the options available for respondents to choose from. The questionnaire is provided in full and would be useful to look at in terms of survey design and administration. The advantage of being able to see the questionnaire is balanced by the minor irritation that there is no index to this edition of the text, which is far too dense to browse for specific information.

Although gender is offered a chapter of its own in the survey results, ethnicity is very rarely mentioned. This is an interesting oversight considering that many of the low paid are from immigrant or ethnic-minority backgrounds. The disabled do not merit significant mention, and the problems of the elderly pensioned are underplayed, possibly for sampling reasons. Given the increasing proportion of the elderly in our society and the fact that poverty is a real threat for many in this group, this is another weakness in the study. This oversight is a function of the sampling process but provides an unbalanced picture.

QUESTIONS

KNOWLEDGE AND UNDERSTANDING

1. Who commissioned the report?
2. What was the social context of the research?
3. What were the aims of this research?
4. What problems are there in operationalising the concept of poverty?
5. Describe the samples used in this study.
6. How did the researchers arrive at the concept of a 'socially perceived necessity'?
7. Why was it necessary for the researchers to supplement their study with official statistics?

ANALYSIS

1. What limitations did the sampling procedure and use of empirical and official data place on the study?
2. Suggest what understandings a qualitative study would bring to a study of poverty in modern Britain.
3. What practical and ethical difficulties are there in producing a large-scale survey of poverty and inequality in our society?

POVERTY AND SOCIAL EXCLUSION IN BRITAIN

David Gordon, Laura Adelman, Karl Ashworth, Jonathan Bradshaw, Ruth Levitas, Sue Middleton, Christina Pantazis, Demi Patsios, Sarah Payne, Peter Townsend and Julie Williams

Joseph Rowntree Foundation, York, 2000

CONTEXT

In 1999 Tony Blair set a target of eradicating child poverty by 2020. His government has also claimed that their policy reforms of the social-security system are designed to tackle poverty. Clearly, if the government is to make a serious attempt to tackle the problem of poverty it needs good research to establish levels of poverty, as well as trends and causes of social exclusion in Britain. This report was intended to offer some kind of baseline for the study of deprivation.

Since 1979 when the New Right gained political ascendancy with the election of the Conservatives and Margaret Thatcher to power in Britain, there had been little serious study of poverty. This was because the New Right either denied the existence of poverty or considered it to be the result of declining cultural and moral values in society. An example of this was illustrated by the key 'please go away' insult phrases of the early 1980s –'On yer bike'. This expression was a mocking reference to a self-help philosophy espoused by leading politician, Norman Tebbit, who remarked that in the 1930s when his own father had been out of work, he had got on his bike and cycled around looking for employment.

The aims of the study were, therefore:

- to re-establish the national tradition of investigating poverty
- to consider the relationship between social exclusion and poverty
- to contribute to global investigation of the phenomena of poverty as agreed by Britain as a signatory to the UN World Summit for Social Development in 1995.

METHODS

This book is intended to update findings of two different surveys that made up the *Breadline Britain* study that is reviewed elsewhere in this volume. The original studies were conducted in 1983 and followed up in 1990. While the first studies were conducted by commercial companies, this study was conducted by a team from four different universities and a government department, the Office for National Statistics.

The survey used similar methods to those of the *Breadline Britain* study to investigate poverty. It measured the number of people who were poor in terms of relative poverty. Were they able to afford items that the majority of the population considered to be necessities? This original methodology was elaborated and expanded from the original survey by adding further questions about other measures of poverty and also of social exclusion. The authors termed the new survey 'PSE', which stands for Poverty and Social Exclusion Survey of Britain.

The method employed here to calculate poverty was a complex set of procedures involving the use of two separate samples – one to suggest necessities and the other to calculate which of these should be used as indicators of deprivation. A third procedure, also based on the two samples, involved the calculation of a poverty threshold that reflected income and the standard of living of respondents. It is claimed that this particular method of calculating poverty has two strong advantages over other methods which have gone before because it:

1. incorporates the views of the general public
2. is based on scientific calculations.

The survey provided two levels of information. It was possible to assess subjective poverty so that we have an understanding of what makes people feel poor, but it also developed this with some understanding of social exclusion. Exclusion is a term that has always been used to *describe* the impact of poverty on individuals and families, but that has been of little practical use until relatively recently in terms of being used to *analyse* the experience of poverty. It is a far wider concept than poverty alone because it looks at the impact of lack of income on life experience and life choice. There are four dimensions to exclusion as operationalised by the research team:

- poverty
- access to employment
- access to services
- access to normal social life and relationships.

The methods used produced a huge array of empirical and statistical data that are analysed in the rest of the report in terms that are accessible and relatively straightforward to understand. There is no subjective data in terms of the quoting of responses such as is found in the *Breadline Britain* survey, but nonetheless, there is measurement of attitudes that gives the material a human dimension.

This study provides a frankly shocking account of the existence and extent of poverty in modern Britain.

ADULT POVERTY IN BRITAIN

Samples of the general public were asked to sort cards containing items and activities relating to their own households and to children. The number of items included was extended from the *Breadline Britain* survey in order to take account of changing living standards. Social activities were included in the sort cards to offer a measure of social exclusion. This process proved significant: the resulting data was a measure of subjective and generally agreed poverty but it could also be used as a baseline for further study. The items used were wide ranging, and mostly a fair reflection of modern British life. Curiously, a dictionary is included in the range of items, with over half of all people surveyed considering this to be a necessity whereas newspapers were generally agreed not to be essentials.

The research team point out that social obligations and customs, such as visits and family celebrations, rank high among necessities. These social obligations sometimes ranked higher than items such as washing machines and high-protein meals three or four times a week. Using this index, just under 28% of people are poor because they were unable to afford two or more necessities. 10% had incomes low enough to make them vulnerable to poverty and others had high enough incomes but were short of some necessities, which suggested that their rise from poverty was recent. The incidence of poverty can depend on the social group to which a person or household belongs and so those who are vulnerable to poverty include women, long-term sick and disabled, retired, lone parents, unemployed, separated or divorced people and non-home owners. Young people are also vulnerable to poverty. One of the main causes of poverty is low income. Some people who were poor by objective measurements of poverty did not feel themselves to be poor subjectively.

The key finding is that '1 in 6 people in a rich industrial society perceive that their incomes are insufficient to meet the very basic needs defined by an absolute poverty threshold'.

CHILD POVERTY IN BRITAIN

Government figures show that over one-third of British children in 1998–89 were living in households with incomes below 50% of the average. The notion of child poverty is a problematic one, however. Evidence suggests that spending on children remains relatively constant throughout the income and social groups so that it would seem that poor parents are depriving themselves of necessities to ensure that their children are cared for. Children's perceptions are not a good basis for poverty analysis because it is not they who make financial decisions about how money can be spent in their homes. Nearly all parents considered new shoes, a coat and fresh fruit or vegetable every day to be necessities, but 2% of children do not have these things. A quarter of all children go without proper birthday celebrations, educational toys, gardens or protein meals. Large numbers have never had a holiday away from home. The children who are vulnerable to deprivation tend to live in lone-parent households, to live in homes where adults are not in full-time work or to be under school age. Some children do not have necessities, not because their parents are on low incomes but because household costs for necessities such as housing and rent are high in some areas. Discussion of government initiatives to reduce poverty by sending parents into the job market suggests that this approach is misguided. Benefits are proportionately higher for small families, but poverty is typical of large families.

GROWTH IN POVERTY

Generally the pattern that emerges is that, taken as a whole, the population of Britain is richer. However, Britain is an increasingly divided society so that the wealthier people have become significantly better off while the poorer people have seen their incomes rise by far less. Respondents expected a higher standard of living and many items that were once seen as luxuries, such as dishwashers, were now seen as necessities. Note, however, that some of these items, such as mobile telephones, are far cheaper to purchase than they were when introduced. Younger adults had a far more sparing view of what was a necessity and ranked clothing items lower than older adults. This may be because many of them experience poverty because they are students or engaged on training schemes.

There have been dramatic rises in the incidence of poverty as measured by lack of socially approved necessities accepted by the bulk of the British population. Poverty now affects 25% of all British households. There are fewer people in long-term poverty so a pattern of people drifting in and out of poverty is emerging.

SOCIAL EXCLUSION

Very large numbers of people in Britain live in households that are jobless: sickness, disability, choice, retirement and caring duties account for the low numbers who work. Traditionally, joblessness has been equated with social exclusion, and for many people, this is indeed true. Poverty can make it difficult for people to meet socially or involve themselves in activities outside the home. This is especially true for those who experience sickness or ill health, the elderly among them. Note that some of those working long hours in low-paid work also experience social exclusion. The research team took a broad view of exclusion, however, and discuss *service exclusion*, which would include items such as bus and train use, or provision of bank and post-office services. *Social exclusion* refers to common activities such as spending time with family or friends. This is important because social contact provides valuable unpaid support such as babysitting. *Exclusion from paid work* is also important in terms of making people isolated and disengaged from normal social contact. Predictably, the unemployed and poorly paid experience significant levels of social exclusion.

It will be interesting to see the impact of this research on government thinking and policy over the next decade or so. The Labour government has been accused of some complacency in terms of its attitudes towards its own record and has set itself a major target of eliminating child poverty within twenty years. It is, however, doing this within the context of a society with ever-widening gaps between the richest and the poorer sectors of the community. Labour's emphasis on adult participation in the social and community life of the nation makes the understanding of exclusion very important. It may well be that this document – which provides a detailed snapshot of British society in 1999 – will be a baseline against which Labour aims can be evaluated.

EVALUATION

The picture that is drawn of the incidence of poverty is dramatic and convincing. Poverty exists at an absolute level and there is widespread secondary poverty in terms of deprivation of socially approved necessities. The term 'social exclusion' has always been a little problematic in sociology because there is no generally agreed definition of what it means. It is a term similar to that of 'underclass' which seems to differ in meaning according to the politics and perspective of the user. Gordon *et al.*, in their attempt to define the term, provide a key service to the study of poverty and exclusion. A quantifiable measure of who is excluded and the reasons for their exclusion from the normal interactions of society are both provided.

Through sophisticated use of the data gathered, Gordon *et al.* were also able to compare and contrast attitudes to poverty in varying social groups so that comparisons between age groups provide sophisticated data.

QUESTIONS

KNOWLEDGE AND UNDERSTANDING

1 Who commissioned the report?
2 What was the social context of the research?
3 What were the aims of this research?
4 What problem is there in operationalising the concept of social exclusion?
5 Why was it significant and necessary to include social obligations and customs in the study?
6 What difficulties are there in determining the extent and experience of poverty among children in Britain?
7 Who is poor in modern Britain?

ANALYSIS

1 What are the implications for this research on government policy? Suggest a variety of approaches as to how governments could tackle issues of poverty and inequality in British society.
2 Suggest reasons why it is important for Governments to have large-scale empirical studies of significant social problems.
3 What practical and ethical difficulties would you experience in producing a qualitative study of social exclusion in British society?

References Gordon, D and Pantazis, C (eds) *Breadline Britain in the 1990s*, Ashgate Publishing, Aldershot

THE IMPACT OF CHILDHOOD DISABILITY ON FAMILY LIFE

Barbara Dobson, Sue Middleton and Alan Beardsworth

Joseph Rowntree Foundation: York, 2001

CONTEXT

Disability is very much a poor relation in a whole range of public, sociological and social-policy debates. Despite the fact that some form of disability is experienced by large numbers of the population (recent figures suggest that as many as 1 in 10 drivers have an orange badge), it is also invisible. It is neglected by the media and ignored by planners; treated as a special case; or seen as problematical in some way. One of the key problems is that disability is often presented in terms of opposition to normal – rather than as an extension of normality or as the extreme end of a continuum, with athletes at one end and the severely physically and or mentally challenged at the other. Individuals with a disability may be seen in terms of the disability rather than their personality and expected to have specific personality traits of 'bitterness', 'heroism' or 'sensitivity' that are associated with handicap. Evidence of this status is in the treatment of film actors who play disabled roles and gain Oscars whilst the genuinely disabled actor may find it difficult to obtain work.

It is also an issue that is clouded by preconceptions of the normal and the misunderstandings of the experts. A common response to disability is one of curiosity, shame or embarrassment. It is a matter of some concern to sociology, and a symptom of the status of the disabled, that one of the key sociological theoretical discussions of attitudes towards the disabled is Erving Goffman's *Stigma*, a study that is nearing its fortieth birthday. This study tackles the issue of disability, not just as a phenomenon in its own right, but as a social and economic issue that needs to be tackled by families. It is grounded in the social reality and lived experiences of those who are affected by the social impact of living with a severely disabled child on a daily basis.

The aims of the study were to:

- investigate the spending patterns of parents of children with a severe disability
- to consider whether parents received sufficient financial support to help them take on caring duties
- to examine some of the emotional costs of bringing up a child with a disability
- to examine the reconstruction of family identity that takes place when a family gains a disabled member.

METHODS

This book was written to explore the financial implications of childhood disability on the family and updates an earlier 1997 study. It also draws on data from Middleton et al.'s (1997) *Small Fortunes* study to find a control group of non-disabled children against which to compare the costs of rearing a disabled child.

The survey used a complex set of procedures to collect its data. In the first instance, it worked from the basic assumption that parents themselves know more about the needs of the family and its disabled member than any other group and the findings were based on their experiences and expertise.

Families were contacted via the Family Fund Trust database. This is an independent trust funded by government that allocates a budget of £20 million each year. The basis for the study was a set of 36 focus groups. These were drawn together so that parents could identify the minimum budget requirements for dealing with childhood disability. In addition, the sessions were taped and parents were allowed to discuss the social and emotional consequences of disability on their lives. In addition, 272 parents completed detailed questionnaires relating to expense, family income, ownership of consumer products, housing, social class and work experiences. 182 parents kept one-week diaries of expenditure. 42 children were also able to complete questionnaires exploring financial issues, including whether they or their siblings did not ask for things because they felt that their parents could not afford it.

There are serious problems in operationalising the concept of disability. The Family Fund Trust database recognises more than 60 conditions. However, the situation is far more complex so that children may experience a range of disabling conditions. Some vary in severity. However, the team focused on the severely handicapped. The study group condensed the conditions into three main groups and then acknowledged that many children could have been placed in either two or all three of the groups:

- mobility-restricted disabilities such as spina bifida
- sensory conditions such as blindness
- traumatic and intermittent conditions such as asthma, epilepsy and autism.

The team tried to organise focus groups on categories of disability so that they could organise and contain the discussion. In practice, the complexity of many children's medical history meant that this attempt did not succeed. Groups were also divided according to age range:

- Birth to 5 years
- 6–10 years
- 11–16 years.

KEY FINDINGS

The focus groups were drawn from four areas of the country, Leicestershire, Derbyshire, Birmingham and Nottingham. The participants in the groups were mostly women. They averaged 36 years of age, but there was considerable variation in the age make-up of the study groups. The groups were less affluent than the general population, but this could have been as a result of having a child with a disability. Many of the households did have consumer durables such as washing machines and central heating in order to cope with the demands made by the child, but some parents, especially single parents, were experiencing serious deprivation.

Spending on a disabled child is variable. Times of ill-health can be financially draining. For many, additional spending on the child amounted to 20% of the household income, a major problem for a family surviving on benefits. The parents spent upwards of £13.50 a week on toys, games and videos for the disabled child. Partly this is prompted for educational and developmental reasons, but also to alleviate boredom or because the toys suited to disabled children are specific to their needs. Books for children with visual impairment cost £10 each. The children were often destructive or obsessive and so items had to be bought rather than borrowed. Clothing is a particular problem because it has excessive wear and needs to be washed frequently. Disabled children require attractive clothes due to the responses of the general public if they are not well dressed. Activities are more necessary for some of these children in order to increase their social contact, but participation is more expensive due to the special facilities required. One telling example is that if children go to leisure centres, they need a parent to accompany them for health and safety reasons as facilities and access are poorly designed and inadequate. The parent is, however, required to pay for a ticket in order to act as an attendant!

Single parents seemed to be spending significantly larger sums that dual families, but nothing the research team discovered could explain this difference fully. Surprisingly, the severity of the disability had little impact on differences in spending levels, expenditure in one area such as special nappies for older severely disabled children could be matched by expenditure in another so that fully mobile children with behaviour or sensory problems required expenditure on activities and toys. In addition, there is the problem that doctors do not like to offer a definite diagnosis for a particular condition until the child is older, but benefits and claims forms require a diagnosis before support can be given. The study suggests that the costs of a disabled child are generally double those of a non-disabled child.

Parents were spending about £65 each week on their children, but by their own assessments of needs, they required a sum nearer to £120 a week. They were having to restrict themselves to very tight budgets and were providing only essential needs. Sometimes the shortfall was taken from other children or the parents themselves were having to do without in order to provide for their disabled children. One respondent had not had a holiday or break for ten years. The benefit system is confusing and disorganised so that some parents were not aware or claiming their full entitlement. The parents had problems in discovering information, filling in forms, being assessed for entitlement and being paid at the incorrect rate. While the benefit situation has improved in recent years, it is still well below what is needed and adds a considerable burden to people who are already experiencing considerable difficulty in the management of their daily lives.

The qualitative area of the study is particularly interesting and shows a pattern of parents and families having to reconstruct their lives with very little support from official agencies. The transition into parenthood is difficult, but for the parents of a disabled child, it is overwhelming because of the fears and worry. In addition, many experienced difficulties with the response of others, one had received almost no birth congratulation cards. They needed to learn strategies to cope with rejection from families and staring by strangers so some had become very assertive in defence of their child's rights. They were not treated as families by professionals, but as 'cases'. This had led to some extraordinarily insensitive and disrespectful behaviour on the part of professional carers such as doctors. Parents tend to view their children as individuals who experience a difficulty, but professionals take a different perspective. They often ignored parental insights and experiences, dismissing them as irrelevant and failing to consult as they saw only the medical or social issues and not the family dimension. As the researcher point out, (p31) '... all said they were tired and exhausted... all of the parents loved their children, some were overwhelmed by the responsibility'.

In addition, life expectations become changed by the presence of a disabled child. Parents had to cope with reduced financial situations, reduced ability to work, and many were passed over for promotion. Many were very concerned by the prospect of retirement or of being outlived by their children. While some extended families had helped and supported the parents of disabled children, other parents had been rejected and so they were having to cope with their own fears and also were supporting grandparents and in-laws in coming to terms with the reality of a disabled grandchild. In order to safeguard themselves, some parents had actually cut contact with their own families and so wider social contacts had disintegrated.

IMPORTANCE

This study is very important as it shows up a major and yet relatively unconsidered weakness in social-service provision. It is actually a fairly damning indictment of care in the community, which for parents of children with severe disability is more probably more accurately termed, 'you're on your own, folks!'. However, this study may not have the impact it deserves to have on the consciousness of the nation because it looks at a topic that many people would prefer to ignore. It is, however, an exemplary combination of qualitative and quantitative study which produces an analysis that is rich in data about the financial and the emotional implications of disability on a family, although presented in cool and scholarly prose.

EVALUATION

In a field where so many professional people such as doctors and social workers have vested career interests in becoming the experts on a disability, parents frequently describe feeling sidelined and ignored by the medical, assessment and educational procedures required. The sociologists who conducted this study have applied a refreshing insight in a situation where so often the disability is seen as a problem for an individual and where only that one person's needs are considered without the family context being considered. This is an important corrective to that situation.

The study team felt confident that the Family Fund Trust database provided a good list of names from which to draw a sample-frame. They estimate that some 60–70% of parents with a disabled child are on this database. There is a social-policy conclusion to be drawn from this; disability is not a serious issue for government if they have no accurate central record. From the point of view of the reliability of the study, the estimates of the quality of the database may be overly optimistic. Given the poverty and disorganisation of information services for families with disabled children it is probable that many have never heard of it or been referred. The team discovered for instance that 3% of families were not even drawing Disability Living Allowance! It is probable that the list is merely the best available source and that it is not fully-representative of all those families with a disabled child.

The sample for such a detailed study was surprisingly large. A further strength of the material is that it avoids the focus on London which is standard for educational studies. Because the groups were all based in regional centres this raises issues about the representativeness of the study, because the impact of geography was not considered. Raising a disabled child in a major urban area is quite a different experience from that of the rural family or one living in an area where the local authority is in extreme financial difficulty.

In its desire to emphasise that the experience of caring for a disabled child is not necessarily a disaster, the study accurately reflects what parents have said about bringing up disabled children but in so doing actually does such parents a mild disservice. The authors point out that the problem for parents is not the disability. The study shows that parents emphasise the personalities of their children and have a surprising resilience and ability to cope with difficult situations. The problem is with the associated difficulties of coping with the related financial difficulty, social isolation and family problems. The study group are careful not to politicise the content of their findings; however, a study that shows that 75% of families with a disabled child are dependent on a single income or on benefits (and that most of the families received income support and were in lower socio-economic groups) suggests that the issue of childhood disability and its impact on family life is barely being touched by government policy.

QUESTIONS

KNOWLEDGE AND UNDERSTANDING

1. Why is disability so under-researched? Suggest three reasons.
2. What were the aims of this research?
3. Describe the sampling procedures and samples used.
4. What problems are there in operationalising the concept of disability?
5. Why are the parents of disabled children less affluent than the rest of the community?
6. Why do parents of disabled children spend more on such children than on non-disabled children?
7. Summarise the problems that parents of disabled children experience from professionals, the own families and the general public.

ANALYSIS

1. What are the implications for this research on government policy? Suggest a variety of approaches governments could use to tackle issues of poverty and inequality among families of disabled children.
2. Evaluate the research under the following headings: reliability, validity, ethics and practicality.
3. What practical and ethical difficulties would you experience in producing a qualitative study of poverty and disability among adults in British society?

References Goffman, E, (1963), *Stigma*, Penguin, Harmondsworth

Middleton, S, Ashworth, K, Braithwaite, I (1997), *Small Fortunes: Spending on Children, Childhood Poverty and Family Sacrifice*, Joseph Rowntree Foundation, York